HIGHLIGHTS FROM
THE BENNINGTON MUSEUM

Edited by
Laura C. Luckey

Entries by
Laura Jane Gombieski
Eugene Kosche
Ruth Levin
Catherine Zusy

The Bennington Museum
West Main Street
Bennington, Vermont 05201

Front cover:
BENNINGTON, 1953
Anna Mary Robertson Moses (Grandma Moses), 1860–1961
© 1989, Grandma Moses Properties Co., New York
See description, Figure 7

Principal Photography:
Blake Gardner, Bennington VT

Photo, p. 26: Nicholas Whitman, North Bennington VT
Photo, p. 30: Eric Borg, Middlebury VT
Photo, p. 74: Helga, NY

Design:
Heidi Humphrey/H Plus, Inc.

Printing:
Sharp Offset Printing, Rutland VT

Typesetting:
Trufont Typographers, Inc.

This publication has been made possible by partial
funding from The National Endowment for the
Arts, Washington, D.C., a Federal Agency.

INTRODUCTION

The Bennington Museum first began as the Bennington Historical Society which was formed in 1875 with a mandate to plan a Centennial celebration for the Battle of Bennington. The plan included not only the building and placement of a battle monument in the Town of Bennington but also the establishment of a museum in which to house and preserve objects and records relating to the early history of the Town.

Although the monument was completed in 1889, it was not until 1923 that plans for the Museum began to materialize. John Spargo, president of the Society, which was then called Bennington Battle Monument and Historical Association, negotiated the purchase of St. Frances de Sales Catholic church which was scheduled for demolition. Built in 1855, the church was bought with funds provided by John Spargo and James C. Colgate and rennovated largely through the financial assistance of Edward H. Everett and James C. Colgate. In 1928 the Bennington Museum was officially opened to the public and today has become one of the major regional museums in New England.

The first Museum collections largely consisted of relics and memorabilia from the Battle of Bennington. However, these were soon joined by other early acquisitions including the portrait of *Captain Elijah Dewey* by Ralph Earl, a windsor writing armchair owned by Ira Allen, and a huge flag acknowledged to be the oldest stars and stripes in America. Among the first benefactors to the Museum were Hall Park McCullough who donated numerous items including a collection of important manuscripts relating to the history of Vermont, and John Spargo, the Museum's first director and curator, who contributed the largest and most comprehensive known collection of Bennington pottery. These men were followed by a succession of generous donors over the years and as the Museum continued to grow it soon became apparent that the building was inadequate to hold the collections. Therefore, in 1937 expansion was undertaken and the name changed to the Bennington Historical Museum and Art Gallery. Finally in 1948 the Institution was incorporated as The Bennington Museum and in that same year received a substantial bequest of paintings, sculpture and decorative arts from Colonel Joseph Colyer, Jr.

Under the leadership of its second director, Richard Carter Barret, the Museum attracted significant additions to the ceramic and glass collections through the gifts of parian and Bennington ware from Elizabeth McCullough Johnson; a major collection of over 1000 goblets from Mr. Norman McColl and an extensive and very important collection of pressed, blown, molded and art glass from Mr. and Mrs. Joseph Limric.

In response to such steady growth, it became necessary for the Museum to be enlarged again and in 1960 a second addition was built followed in 1974 by further expansion which brought the building to its present size and included a gallery named in honor of Esther Merrill Parmelee. Although the primary collections relate to military history and the development of the Town together with 19th century glass and ceramics, the Museum has grown dramatically over the years. Today the collections include notable examples of 18th and 19th century American furniture and paintings as well as silver and other decorative arts. There are textiles which range from costumes, quilts and samplers to a wide variety of accessories in addition to dolls and toys, trade signs and weathervanes. The Museum also owns an antique touring car called the Wasp, which was made in Bennington in 1924, and has on permanent view an unparalled public collection of paintings by the revered folk artist, Grandma Moses who grew up and worked in nearby New York State.

Now, 61 years later the Museum stands tall among its peers strongly supported by a dedicated membership and the generosity of many donors who have helped the collection to grow not only in size but in stature. It is the foresight and generosity and vision of the Museum's benefactors that have preserved not only the history but also the art of this community, of Vermont and of New England and left us with this proud and important heritage.

ACKNOWLEDGEMENTS

In addition to the authors listed on the title page, special thanks must also be extended to Kirk Nelson who contributed four of the entries and was largely responsible for the successful grant from the National Endowment for the Arts which partially funded this publication. Photographer Blake Gardner worked tirelessly to achieve the fine illustrations presented here and was assisted by the curatorial staff together with building manager, Jack Coyne and his assistants, Patrick Griffin and Ned Mulligan. Anita Gauthier copy edited the entire manuscript with meticulous care and Lisa Jolin typed all the entries as they moved through various stages and revisions to completion. Finally, we recognize the many scholars both past and present, whose research, knowledge and insights have informed this catalogue.

—L.C.L.

Fig. 1   Fig. 2

Figures 1 and 2.
PAUL BRIGHAM and LYDIA SAWYER BRIGHAM, ca. 1802
William Jennys
American, active 1795–1810
Oil on canvas
30½ × 24¼ in.
Gifts of Mrs. Arthur L. Douglass and Mrs. Mary Brigham Loud

Paul Brigham served as a Captain under George Washington in the Revolutionary Army and fought in the battles of Germantown and Monmouth. Born in Coventry, Ct. in 1746, Brigham and his wife moved to Norwich, Vt. in 1798. A solid statesman and diplomat, Brigham served for 22 years in the State legislature under both federalist and democratic governors first as a Councillor, then as Lt. Governor and, finally, he was named acting Governor from August 25–October 16, 1797, following the death of Governor Chittenden.

In Federal America, as in Colonial times, portraiture was the predominant theme of painting and a demand for likenesses prevailed in rural areas as well as in large cities. As a result, itinerant artists such as William Jennys travelled extensively painting portraits of prominent citizens. Despite his lack of formal training, Jennys produced over 100 portraits which are astonishingly accurate in their characterization of the sitters. Between 1795–1800 Jennys worked in several western Connecticut towns, moved up the Connecticut valley into Massachusetts and by 1802 was in Vermont. The carefully delineated forms and strongly modelled features are typical of Jennys' realistic style which far surpassed many of his contemporaries. This pair of portraits of Mr. and Mrs. Brigham were probably painted in Norwich, Vt. ca. 1802 when Jennys was known to have been in Vermont.

—R.L.

Figure 3.
WOMAN IN WHITE (Grace Harrison Hatch), 1906
Lorenzo Hatch
American 1856–1914
Oil on Canvas
78 × 38 in.
Signed and dated lower left: L.J. Hatch 1906
Gift of the Hatch Estate

Lorenzo Hatch first came to Dorset, Vt. as a young boy, and lived opposite the Dorset Cemetery with his widowed mother and two sisters. At the age of 14, Hatch was apprenticed to watchmaker, Charles Whitcomb, of nearby Salem, New York, from whom he learned the art of engraving, and soon demonstrated a remarkable talent by producing an impressive engraving of the head of George Washington.

In 1874 George B. McCartee, Chief of the U.S. Bureau of Engraving and Printing, saw Hatch's engraving of Washington, and recommended that the young artist be apprenticed to the Bureau. In 1887, Hatch left that government post to work for the Western Bank Note and Engraving Company in Chicago and two years later joined the International Bank Note Company in New York. While there, Hatch also studied with Robert Henri at the New School of Art where he turned his attention to portrait and landscape painting. Despite his travels, Hatch returned each summer to Dorset where he founded an art colony which in the late 1950's became the Southern Vermont Art Center located in Manchester, Vt. Although Hatch exhibited his work, he refused to sell any pictures during his lifetime and it was only after his death that, in addition to his reputation as an engraver and printer, he became recognized as a painter.

In 1894, Hatch met Grace Harrison at the Chicago World's Fair; she became his wife, and is the sitter for this portrait. At the invitation of the Chinese Government, Hatch was asked to establish the Bureau of Engraving and Printing in Peking, China in 1908. In November of that year, he, his wife and one son left for China with Hatch's associate, the engraver, William Grant. Despite political upheavals, Hatch fulfilled his contract and remained in China with his family until his death, after which his body was escorted to Dorset by two officials of the Chinese government.

—R.L.

Figure 4.
MAY SUYDAM PALMER, 1901
Frederick W. MacMonnies
American, 1863–1937
Oil on Canvas
82 × 42½ in.
Signed l.l. with monogram of Pegasus
Gift of Courtland Palmer

Frederick William MacMonnies was born in Brooklyn, N.Y. and, as a young man, studied in Manhattan at the Cooper Union, the National Academy of Design, and the Art Students League. In 1881, MacMonnies worked as a studio assistant with the well-known sculptor, Augustus Saint-Gaudens and later with architects McKim, Mead and White on decorations for the Cornelius Vanderbilt II residence in New York. He left for Paris in 1884 where he studied at the Ecole des Beaux Arts. Known primarily as a sculptor, MacMonnies, early in his career, established a style marked by realism and naturalistic forms which bore little resemblance to the neoclassical style still popular during that period.

Fig. 4

Fig. 3

In 1887, MacMonnies opened a studio in Paris, then turned briefly to painting in 1900 when he produced portraits such as this one, which was almost certainly done in nearby Giverny, of *May Palmer* (1870–1941), who was herself a painter. At the time MacMonnies wrote to his student, Mary Foote, that Miss Palmer "begged me to paint her portrait. . . . I am going to paint Miss P. if the sun holds out in the late afternoon— sunset on her red hair—and blown around in her best Chinese gown, toss't by the winds on the alley walk to Monet's boathouse." In 1905, MacMonnies opened an art school in Giverny, a favorite gathering place for the French Impressionists whose work clearly had a strong influence on him during this time. MacMonnies returned to sculpture in 1906 with even greater enthusiasm and conviction; however, in 1916, as a result of World War I, he came back to the United States and again took up painting.

Another large painting by MacMonnies, in the collection of The Bennington Museum, is of Mary Sartell Prentice shown full length on the porch of her house in Old Bennington. Painted in 1902, this portrait also bears the Pegasus monogram. This symbol was used by MacMonnies in homage to his close friend James McNeill Whistler, who signed his paintings with a butterfly monogram.

—R.L.

7

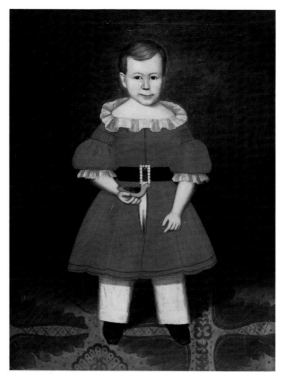

Fig. 5

Figure 5.
LUMAN PRESTON NORTON, ca. 1840
Erastus Salisbury Field
American, 1805–1900
Oil on canvas
43½ × 33¼ in.
Joseph H. Colyer, Jr. Purchase Fund

Luman Preston Norton (1847–1906) was the son of Julius Norton and great-grandson of Captain John Norton, founder of the Norton Pottery in 1793. This painting is not only one of Field's finest portraits of a young child, it is also significant to the documentation of the Norton family. "Little Lumie" as he is known by those closely associated with the Museum, is one of six known portraits of children in which similar carpets appear with large red and green pattern variations on a light brown background. Other characteristics of Field's work, such as the heavy outlining of face, hands and arms and having his sitters hold an object, are also evident in this portrait. Although the bird held by Luman is probably carved and painted wood, family tradition states he would not stand still for his portrait unless he was allowed to hold his bird.

Luman was the first college graduate to enter the family business and went into partnership with his father in 1859 when he was 22 years old. He worked with his father until his father's death in 1861 after which he became manager of the Pottery in partnership with Edward Norton, his father's cousin. In 1881 Luman sold his interest in the business to Edward and devoted his energies to his position as President of the Bennington County Savings Bank.

—R.L.

Fig. 6

Figure 6.
JULIUS NORTON, ca. 1840
Erastus Salisbury Field
American, 1805–1900
Oil on canvas
35 × 29 in.
Gift of Dorothy Norton Payson and her Children

Julius Norton, (1809–1861), was a gifted member of the well-known Norton family which made pottery in Bennington, Vt. for over 100 years. The grandson of Captain John Norton, founder of the famous Norton Pottery, Julius carried on the family tradition. Educated at the Bennington Academy, he worked first with his father, Luman Norton before going into partnership with his brother-in-law, Christopher Webber Fenton, from 1844 to 1847. He took over the management of the Pottery in 1847. Reputed to be the best flutist in Bennington County, Julius Norton also played the piano and violin, and was described in his day as "universally respected, honored and upright."

Erastus Salisbury Field was born in Leverett, Mass. in 1805 and, after training with Samuel F.B. Morse, a painter best known for his invention of the telegraph, worked as an itinerant artist painting portraits throughout Massachusetts and Connecticut. In 1839, Field travelled first to Brattleboro, Vt., and then to Bennington where he painted portraits of several members of the Norton family, four of which are in The Bennington Museum. Two years later, he moved to New York where he is listed as a resident until 1848 when he returned to his family homestead in Leverett. Although Field's earlier work is characterized by hard-edged, somewhat flat figures which usually appear against an empty background with a halo effect surrounding the heads, his portraits after 1850 were almost all painted directly from photographs and, as a result, appear more realistic and often include background detail. Throughout his career, which spanned most of the 19th century, Field's work remained strong, colorful and imposing. As portraiture became more and more the province of the

Fig. 7

photographers, he turned his attention almost exclusively to painting historical and religious subjects. Field cast his vote in the Massachusetts State election just before his 95th birthday and was the oldest man in Franklin County when he died on June 28, 1900.

—R.L.

Figure 7.
BENNINGTON, 1953
Anna Mary Robertson Moses (Grandma Moses)
American, 1860–1961
Oil on pressed wood
18 × 24 in.
Signed l.r. MOSES
Museum Purchase

Anna Mary Robertson Moses, better known as Grandma Moses, was born in Greenwich, New York, not far from Bennington, Vermont. At the age of 75 she began to paint and in 1940 had her first one man show in New York City at the Galerie St. Etienne. Grandma Moses' work immediately gained national attention at a time when a strong interest in folk art was growing in the United States. In the 1950s and '60s her paintings were shown in several European countries including Germany, Austria, Switzerland, France, England and the U.S.S.R. and during these years she received numerous awards and honorary degrees. When Grandma Moses died in 1961 she was 101. Within 25 years she had become an internationally known artist acclaimed throughout the world for her unique views of upper New York state.

Bennington was painted at the height of Grandma Moses' career and combines details that are both real and remembered. The gray building of The Bennington Museum with its 1937 addition is shown at the center of the picture located just to the left of the Bennington Battle Monument, and is the only instance in which a museum appears in one of Grandma Moses' paintings. However, the horse-drawn wagons and carts refer to an earlier time and describe the kind of transportation that would have existed when Grandma Moses was a young girl and which she chose to include instead of the cars and trucks that were fast invading her quiet, pristine world. Although Grandma Moses painted over 1500 known works, very few depict specific towns such as this view of Bennington. Instead, the countryside surrounding her farm in Eagle Bridge, New York close to the border of southern Vermont, became the setting for most of her paintings.

During her astonishing career, Grandma Moses made an impact on thousands of people who were touched by the simplicity and special character of the scenes and activities she recorded. She captured the spirit of traditional pastimes such as apple butter and cider making, maple sugaring, sleigh rides in winter or simply the still beauty of a snow covered village or spring planted fields. Few artists of this century ever enjoyed the remarkable success during their lifetime that Grandma Moses had. Today her work is still prized and her paintings continue to delight people of all ages throughout the world.

Another view of Bennington by Grandma Moses in the Museum's collection, painted in 1945 from a panoramic photograph, shows the commercial and industrial aspects of the town in the early part of the century.

—L.C.L.

Figure 8.
THE ROMAN GIRL, ca. 1866
William Morris Hunt
American, 1824–1879
Oil on Canvas
48 × 23 in.
Signed on skirt W.M.H. (in monogram)
Gift of George Adams Ellis

William Morris Hunt was born in Brattleboro, Vt. and descended from a long line of illustrious Vermonters including his father, Jonathan Hunt, who was a judge and representative to Congress, and two famous brothers, the architect, Richard Morris Hunt, and photographer, Leavitt Hunt.

As a young man Hunt studied drawing briefly in New Haven, Ct., before traveling to Italy with his family where he worked for a short time in Rome prior to entering the Dusseldorf Academy in 1846. From 1847 to 1852, Hunt studied in Paris with Thomas Couture. Although Couture's influence is evident in Hunt's early work it was the French painter, Jean Francois Millet with whom Hunt studied in 1853, who was to have the most profound impact on both the subject matter and style

Fig. 8

Fig. 9

of Hunt's work. Hunt's friendship with Millet and his relationship with other French painters in Barbizon such as Corot, led to his promotion of their work in Boston. When Hunt settled in Boston in 1862, it was his enthusiasm for the Barbizon painters that led Bostonians to be among the earliest patrons and collectors of their paintings and of Millet's work, in particular.

Hunt was a versatile artist and worked in many mediums producing portraits, landscapes, and drawings as well as the large important murals of *Anahita, Flight of Night*, completed about 1878 for the Capitol building in Albany, N.Y. *The Roman Girl* shown here closely resembles a sketch of the same subject in the Metropolitan Museum in New York which is signed and dated 1866 and which was, without doubt, drawn on Hunt's second trip to Europe in that year. Another painting, *The Italian Girl* in the Boston Museum of Fine Arts dated 1867 shows a bust length portrait of the same model.

—R.L.

Figure 9.
TOWNSCAPE OF BENNINGTON, 1798
Ralph Earl
American, 1751–1801
Oil on Canvas
36 × 60 in.
Museum Purchase

The landscape paintings of Ralph Earl are among the earliest and finest examples of the genre which, with the emergence of the Hudson River School in the late 1820s, became one of the most vital movements in 19th century American art. During the late 18th century, landscape scenes appeared most typically in portrait backgrounds and depicted the residence or property of the sitter. Earl's landscape paintings stand out, therefore, as significant exceptions to the general practice.

Earl was born in Worcester, Mass., and began his painting career in New Haven, Ct., shortly before the outbreak of the American Revolution. Motivated by loyalist sympathies, Earl left America for London in 1778, where he studied with Benjamin West and exhibited portraits at The Royal Academy. Following his return to America in 1785, Earl travelled throughout New England and achieved recognition as one of the foremost American portraitists of that era.

In 1798 his travels brought him to Bennington, Vt., where he painted the portraits of *Mary Schenck Dewey* and her husband, *Captain Elijah Dewey*. Dewey's imposing gambrel-roofed house is featured in the background of his portrait, and reappears in the *View of Bennington* also painted by Earl. Other buildings visible in the landscape that still stand include the Governor Isaac Tichenor homestead in the center foreground, the Parson Jedediah Dewey house at the far right, and the General David Robinson house half way up the hill to the present site of the Bennington Battle Monument. To the left of the Robinson house and directly above the Tichenor homestead stands the first courthouse in Bennington County, which burned down in 1809. Earl's monumental view of Bennington represents one of his finest landscape efforts, provides historians with an invaluable record of the town, and contains the only known self-portrait of the artist, who appears busily sketching in the left foreground.

—K.N.

Figures 10 and 11.
CAPTAIN ELIJAH DEWEY and
MARY SCHENCK VAN DER SPIEGEL McEOWEN DEWEY, 1798
Ralph Earl
American, 1751–1801
Oil on canvas
45½ × 35½ in.; 30½ × 24¾
Signed l.l. R. EARL pinxt 1798
Museum purchase funds raised by public subscription and given in memory of Gertrude Cuyster
Hubbell, 1911; and, Gift of Laura Merrill Penniman and John Merrill

Captain Elijah Dewey, the son of the first minister in Bennington, the Reverend Jedidiah Dewey, was born in Westfield, Mass., in 1744 and died in Bennington in 1818. Dewey is shown in this portrait with the present-day Walloomsac Inn located on Monument Avenue, Old Bennington, in the background. For over 40 years, Dewey was proprietor of the Inn which was originally known as Dewey's Tavern. He led a very active life, serving as a Captain of the Bennington militia at Ticonderoga in 1776, in Bennington and Saratoga in 1777, and hosting many revolutionary and political meetings in his Inn. One famous occasion took place at the Inn in 1791 when the U.S. Secretary of State, Thomas Jefferson, and Virginia Congressman, James Madison, both destined to become U.S. Presidents, paid an official visit to the town.

Mary Schenck, born in 1756, was twice widowed when she married her third husband, Captain Elijah Dewey, proprietor of the Walloomsac Inn, in 1792. She died in 1820 only two years after the death of Captain Dewey.

—R.L.

Fig. 10

Fig. 11

Figure 12.

TALL CASE CLOCK, 1793
Daniel Burnap, 1759–1838
East Windsor, Connecticut
Cherry and Pine
H: 93 in. L: 21½ in. W: 11 in.

Daniel Burnap served his apprenticeship with Thomas Harland (1735–1807), a prominent English clockmaker who arrived in America in 1773, and settled in Norwich, Ct. where he established his shop. Although small, Harland's shop became America's first watch and clock factory producing about 200 watches and 40 clocks a year. As a result of training craftsmen such as Burnap, Harland's shop had a profound influence on the American manufacture of clocks.

In 1780, Burnap established his own shop in East Windsor, Ct., which soon became a small factory producing a substantial number of clocks as well as numerous hardware items, surveying instruments and related accessories. As was customary, Burnap also trained many apprentices who made up a large part of his work force, nearly all of whom became successful clockmakers. Burnap's most outstanding apprentice was Eli Terry who, by 1830, became the world's largest manufacturer of machine-made clocks, in East Windsor, Ct., establishing Connecticut as the clockmaking center of the world. As Harland's shop before him, Burnap's small factory also produced engraved brass, and plain or silvered clock dials which were the first to be made in America and sold to the trade on a regular basis.

Although most of Burnap's cases were obtained from other cabinetmakers in the area, his shop records indicate that in 1795 he had a casemaker at his shop for a short time who produced 22 cases in 18 weeks; yet only a third of Burnap's clocks were sold with cases. His records also note that the clock illustrated here was sold without a case to General Paul Brigham of Norwich, Vt. in June, 1793. In October of that same year, Burnap traded two eight-day brass clocks to cabinetmaker Hezekiah

Fig. 12

Fig. 13

Kelly of Norwich, Vt. for seven clock cases. It is therefore quite possible that Kelly also made the case for this clock.

The clocks of Daniel Burnap exhibit not only fine craftsmanship but also timekeeping accuracy, as Burnap frequently used the expensive, but superior, "dead beat" escapement invented by the English clockmaker George Graham in 1715. In 1796, Burnap moved to Coventry, Ct. and, according to his records, by 1805, had virtually retired from clockmaking. From that time until his death in 1838 at the age of 78, Burnap's activities centered around his sawmill and various township positions.

—E.K.

Figure 13.
ARMCHAIR
Probably Connecticut or Vermont, early 19th century
Curly maple, rush seat
H: 33¾ in. W: 19½ in. D: 20 in.
Bequest of Mrs. Esther Dewey Merrill Parmelee

This armchair is a delightful curly maple rendition of a Sheraton "fancy chair" with its characteristic pillow-back crest rail, elaborately turned legs, scrolled arms and rush seat. "Fancy chairs," sometimes called Hitchcock chairs after the well-known Connecticut painted chairs made by Lambert Hitchcock, were inexpensive alternatives to the more formal carved and upholstered furniture of the Federal and Empire periods.

The accomplished maker of this chair used the irregular pattern and lively rippled surface of local curly maple, in place of painted decoration, to enhance the appearance of the chair. He also took liberties with the design of the back stay rail, where instead

Fig. 14

of the more popular motifs of the eagle, horn of plenty or basket of fruit, an abstracted design was used resembling the elaborately carved crest rails and front stretchers of American- made William and Mary chairs. In addition, the blocked and turned legs as well as hoofed feet on this chair are unusual features.

Curly maple fancy chairs of similar designs are known to have been made in the Hartford and Middletown areas of Connecticut in the early 1800s. Therefore, it is possible that this chair, which has a Bennington provenance, may have come from Connecticut, as furniture was regularly transported up the Connecticut River to Vermont or, it could be the product of a local Connecticut-trained craftsman. At least one chairmaker working in Bennington, Henry F. Dewey, advertised the sale of maple fancy chairs from the late 1820s until the 1840s (see p. 18). Although it appears that this chair was made between 1820 and 1840, it was thought to have been owned by Captain Elijah Dewey (1744–1818), a prominent military and civic leader in Bennington (see p. 13).

—C.Z.

Figure 14.
SACK-BACK WINDSOR CHAIR WITH WRITING ARM
New England, late 18th–early 19th century
Painted hickory, ash and pine
H: 38½ in. W: 29 in. D: 31 in.
Purchased by the Bennington Battle Monument and Historical Society

According to tradition, this Windsor writing chair was owned by Ira Allen (1751–1814), brother of Ethan Allen, the famous leader of the Green Mountain Boys.

First trained as a surveyor, Ira Allen, explored and mapped out vast areas of the New Hampshire grants and became owner of large expanses of the new territory. He also served as a Lieutenant in Seth Warner's regiment with the Green Mountain Boys, represented his town of Colchester in all the conventions of the New Hampshire grants in 1776 and 1777, and played a principal role in drafting the Constitution of the Republic of Vermont. Ira Allen also designed the Vermont State seal and served as the Republic's Treasurer, Surveyor-General and member of the Governor's Council in the late 1770s. In 1798, he published *The Natural and Political History of the State of Vermont, One of the United States of America*, which is still one of the most valuable early histories of the state.

Windsor chairs, inexpensive and made of common and mixed woods, were in wide use during the late 18th and early 19th centuries. Thomas Jefferson drafted the Declaration of Independence sitting in a Windsor chair, Benjamin Franklin sat in a Windsor chair at Independence Hall, and George Washington seated his parlor guests at Mount Vernon in Windsor chairs. Because they were made from a variety of woods, the chairs were usually painted first with an undercoat of pink or light colored wash and then given a final coat of either dark green, black, red, brown, or yellow. Hickory was commonly used to make the spindles, tulip or pine the seat, maple the legs, and either oak or ash the bow of the back. The chair shown here made of hickory, ash and pine, was originally painted red with a light undercoat of pink.

The bamboo turnings on this chair are characteristic of those made in New London County, Ct. around 1800. It is possible that a Connecticut-trained craftsman made this chair either in Connecticut or in Vermont where Ira Allen lived primarily from 1773 until 1803.

—C.Z.

Figure 15.
ROCKING CHAIR, 1838
Henry Freeman Dewey, 1800–1882, Bennington, Vermont
Curly, plain and birds-eye maple, pine seat
H: 44¼ in. W: 23½ in. D: 29 in.
Inscribed in pencil on seat bottom: H.F. Dewey/Chairmaker/East Bennington/Sept. 15, 1838/1838/$4.50
Gift of Patricia Blackmer Thibodeau

The rocker, apparently an American invention, evolved from a combination of the cradle and easy chair, and was used in the colonies as early as 1740. While the first rockers were slat-back or Windsor chairs with rockers added, the form had become so popular by 1820 that chairmakers were producing them commercially as a stock item. Henry F. Dewey, the maker of this arrow-back Windsor rocker, was one of hundreds of chairmakers who were providing rockers for the people in their communities. Although the majority of Dewey's rockers were not labelled, branded or otherwise marked, this chair bears a full pencilled inscription noting not only the name of the maker, but the location and date of manufacture and price. The chair features the flat convex front stretcher which is characteristic of Dewey's work.

Born in Connecticut, Henry F. Dewey was one of a few chairmakers working in Bennington in the 1820s. By 1827, he was in partnership with a Mr. Woodworth and had established a chair factory on East Main Street which not only sold rockers, but also "fancy" and Windsor chairs as well as settees, which were offered "as low as can be bought at any shop in the country." According to an advertisement in the *Vermont*

Fig. 15

Gazette, Dewey's shop employed the finest craftsmen who worked in the most fashionable, modern style. In addition to making chairs, many of them of local maple, the shop did repair work as well as varnishing and painting. Dewey also sold his chairs to other merchants, including Stephen and Edward Pratt of Bennington, and sold other chairmakers' products in his shop as well. In 1841, he advertised that he had just received "a large assortment of cane bottom chairs in the latest New York style. WARRENTED A GOOD ARTICLE."

Dewey maintained a dry goods shop and held many public offices in the community including deputy sheriff, constable, tax collector, and overseer of the poor. Later, he became an official with the United States Pottery and, in 1863, reopened part of the pottery, which had closed in 1858, to grind feldspar on a small scale for other potteries.

Dewey's account book reveals that he was a better craftsmen than businessman as he noted repeatedly that accounts were "settled but not honest," "settled by my over-paying," and even "settled by Kings leaving and not paying."

—C.Z.

Fig. 16

Figure 16.

MUSICAL TALL CASE CLOCK,
ca. 1808
Nichols Goddard, 1773–1823
Rutland, Vermont
Mahogany and pine
H: 94¼ in. W: 19½ in. D: 9¼ in.
Museum Purchase

Musical tall clocks represent the highest achievement of the 18th century clock-maker's domestic production, and fewer than 100 American examples are known to survive. In their first advertisement, placed in the *Rutland Herald* of July 3, 1797, the partnership of Benjamin Lord and Nichols Goddard listed musical clocks along with gold beads and rings, silver spoons, buckles, buttons and sugar tongs. Benjamin Lord provided the partnership with its silversmithing skills. A native of Norwich, Ct., he first advertised his trade in Pittsfield, Mass., in 1796, and a year later had joined Goddard in Rutland. Their partnership was dissolved within 10 years; however, Lord continued his trade there until 1831 when he moved to Athens, Ga.

According to Nichols Goddard, Jr., his father learned the trade of clockmaking in Shrewsbury, Mass., where he was born. At least two musical tall clocks made during the time of the Goddard/Lord partnership remained in the possession of the Goddard family in 1886, when Nichols, Jr. published a newspaper account of his family recollections. He states the clocks played one tune each day of the week, with a psalm reserved for Sundays, and "in the manufacture of these clocks there was a fine hand-engine or milling machine used by Goddard for cutting gears and pinions." Both Lord and Goddard were respected businessmen in Rutland, active free-masons who held important positions in town government.

A musical clock such as this would have been one of the most prized posses-sions in the household, valued at up to $70 or $80 and second only to the fully fur-nished bed as a sign of affluence and taste. Fine examples of tall clocks by Lord and

Fig. 17

Goddard can be seen in the collections of the Sheldon Museum, Middlebury, Vt., and the Albany Institute of Art. Made after the partnership dissolved, The Bennington Museum's clock is one of only two musical examples known to exist.

—K.N.

Figure 17.
BLANKET CHEST WITH DRAWERS
South Shaftsbury, Vermont, early 19th century
Painted white pine
H: 41 in. W: 41⅛ in. D: 19¼ in.
Museum Purchase

Country cabinetmakers often painted their simple pine furniture with decorative designs or to resemble the grain of more exotic and expensive woods. This chest, which is almost identical in size and form to one signed "Thomas Matteson/S. Shaftsbury, Vermont/1824" in the collection of the Henry Ford Museum, and is painted in the style of several other chests found in Southern Vermont, may have been made by the same craftsman.

Whether Thomas Matteson was the owner or maker of the Henry Ford Museum's chest is difficult to assess. There are three other related painted blanket chests which are signed: "By J. Matteson/August 1 A.D. 1803," (collection of Historic Deerfield, Inc.), "Benoni Matteson to B. Burlingame Dr./To Paint $2.70/To Paint & Grain Chest 2.00/$4.70" (private collection), and "Thomas G. Matison/South

Fig. 18

Shaftsbury/V.t [sic]/1824" (ex-collection of Henry Ford Museum). The inscriptions on these chests suggest that a number of members of the Matteson family of South Shaftsbury were making and/or painting furniture, and might have owned it. Searches through local church and land records, Bennington County's *Vermont Gazette,* and probate inventories have as yet failed to provide any conclusive evidence about the maker(s) of this furniture.

The construction of the Museum's chest with its thick, rough cut, pine boards and irregular dove tails, suggests that it was not the product of a trained cabinetmaker, but, perhaps, was made by a farmer or woodworker who filled the long winters constructing and decorating furniture. Like many rural craftsmen, the maker of this chest appears to have had little interest in keeping up with fashion. The blanket chest was a traditional form, more common to the 17th and 18th centuries than the 19th century, when this one was made.

—C.Z.

Figure 18.
SIDEBOARD, ca. 1798
Possibly Julius Barnard, 1769–after 1812, of Northampton, Massachusetts; New Hampshire; Windsor, Vermont; and Montreal, Canada; or Elijah Pomroy of Hanover, New Hampshire
Mahogany crotch veneer with maple, birch, satinwood and walnut inlays; secondary woods are pine and cherry
H: 40 in. W: 62 in. D: 27⅞ in.
Gift of Miss Henrietta G. Storer

An outstanding example of Federal style in both design and craftsmanship, this
sideboard was purchased by Elijah West as a wedding gift in 1798 for his daughter,

Sophia (b. 1778) and his business partner, Allen Hayes (1756–1831). At the time, West owned both a dry goods store and a tavern in Windsor, Vt. where the State Constitution was drafted in 1777, which led to the legendary description of this piece as "the Constitution House sideboard." According to Museum records, soon after their marriage, the Hayes' built a fine residence, in which this casepiece was used, near the Constitution House. It remained in the Hayes family until 1947 when it was given to the Museum by Miss Henrietta G. Storer, the great-granddaughter of Allen and Sophia West Hayes.

The sideboard, a form that developed in the 1770s in England, was first published in George Hepplewhite's *The Cabinetmaker and Upholster's Guide* in 1778 and became popular in America in the 1790s. As America prospered in the early 1800s, successful merchants built grand Federal period houses which were furnished in the latest fashion. It is not surprising therefore that the residents of Windsor, one of the largest towns in Vermont between 1800 and 1810, and a center for milling and manufacturing, would also chose classically inspired furniture for their houses.

By the early 1800s, cabinetmakers in Windsor were producing some of the finest Federal furniture in the state. Julius Barnard, a New York-trained cabinetmaker from Northampton, Mass., who moved to the Windsor area in 1801, may have made this sideboard. In Windsor's *Post Boy* in 1805, he advertised that his shop could produce over 25 different furniture forms, including sideboards, and is known to have made a sideboard of similar quality and construction which is now in the collection of the Hood Museum at Dartmouth College. Elijah Pomroy of Hanover, N.H. (just across the river from Windsor), also advertised "all kinds of Mahogany and Cherry Furniture may be had, in the newest fashions, and on the shortest notice—viz. Side-Boards," and illustrated a sideboard almost identical to this one, in the *Dartmouth Gazette* in 1803.

—C.Z.

Figure 19.
HIGH CHEST OF DRAWERS, 1775–1790
Made by the shop of Major John Dunlap, 1746–1792, or Lieutenant Samuel Dunlap, 1752–1830
Goffstown, Bedford or Henniker, New Hampshire
Maple, pine
H: 85¾ in. W: 41½ in. D: 21½ in.
Bequest of Mrs. Esther Dewey Merrill Parmelee

Major John Dunlap (1746–1792) and his brother Lieutenant Samuel Dunlap (1752–1830), made furniture and panelled interiors in Southern New Hampshire during the late 18th and early 19th centuries.

Although the Dunlaps had access to urban centers and formal traditions of cabinetwork, they chose to create their own designs and developed a distinctive regional style of cabinetry. This high chest is characteristic of their work as seen by the basket weave cornice, heavy upper moldings, abundant surface decoration featuring several shells or sunbursts, s-shaped scrolls on a deep skirt, and short legs. Also common to the Dunlap's work are the visual tricks of making a single long drawer look like three smaller ones as seen on the second drawer from the top and the bottom drawer. In addition, the top drawer of the lower case has been made to look like two drawers. The juxtaposition of the shell carvings on the top center drawers, may be unique to this chest.

Fig. 19

The furniture produced by the Dunlaps and the craftsmen in their shops was primarily made of local hardwoods such as maple, pine, birch and cherry, rather than the more expensive imported mahogany used by urban craftsmen in major furniture-making centers such as Boston, Newport and Philadelphia.

This high chest of drawers relates to chests in the collection of the New Hampshire Historical Society and the Henry Francis du Pont Winterthur Museum, both of which are documented as being made in the shop of Major John Dunlap in the early 1780s.

—C.Z.

Fig. 20

Figure 20.
JOINED CHEST WITH DRAWERS, 1700–1725
Probably Hatfield or Hadley, Massachusetts
Oak, pine
H: 38¾ in. W: 46 in. D: 19½ in.
Initials carved on front center panel: A. W.
Bequest of Mrs. Gertrude D. Webster

Distinguished by overall flat-carved decoration of oak leaves and lobed tulips, incised scrolls and punched backgrounds, "Hadley" chests were made by joiners working in shops along the Connecticut River Valley from Northfield, Mass. to Enfield and Suffield, Ct. between 1700 and 1725. Approximately 175 panelled chests, chests of drawers as well as boxes and tables have been identified with these decorative motifs which comprise the largest group of carved 17th century American furniture known with related ornamentation. The floral carving on the surface of these chests, probably an interpretation of Renaissance decoration, was practiced by carvers from the Lake District in northern England during the 17th century who brought this carving tradition with them when they came to America.

Hadley chests, so named by collector Henry Wood Erving who found a similar one in Hadley, Massachusetts in 1883, were made as dowry chests or wedding gifts, and usually bear the carved initials and ocassionally the name of the owner. Early research conducted on them in the first half of the 19th century has suggested that the initials A. W. on this chest might stand for *Abbie Wyman*. According to tradition, it was brought up the Connecticut River on a flat boat by the Ely family and found in Ascutneyville, Vt. around 1875. It is the earliest known piece of furniture in the Museum's collection and was probably originally painted black or red as was typical of most Hadley chests.

—C.Z.

Fig. 21

Figure 21.

CHEST ON CHEST, 1770–1800
Essex County; probably Salem, Marblehead or Newburyport, Massachusetts
Mahogany, white pine
H: 83 in. W: 44 in. D: 22¼ in.
Largely illegible chalk inscription on bottom of lower case drawer: . . . S John . . .
Bequest of Mrs. Gertrude D. Webster (ex-collection of Charles D. Davenport)

This stately chest illustrates the shallow blocking, high-broken scroll pediment and carved center shell at the base of which are characteristics of casepieces found on the north shore of Massachusetts primarily in the towns of Salem, Beverly and Marblehead.

The block-front form characterized by richness of wood, classical proportions and symmetry, originated in Boston in the 1730s, and continued to be popular among the merchant class largely in Boston, Mass. and Newport, R.I. throughout the 18th century. The decorative blocking on these great chests, requiring the use of imported thick, mahogany boards which were then cut away and carved to create this surface design, made them among the most costly furniture forms produced at this time.

During the 18th century, coastal towns in Essex County, Massachusetts, prospered from shipbuilding and fishing which resulted in new wealth and a greater demand for such fine furniture as the chest shown here. As a result, the cabinetmaking trade flourished, with Thomas Chippendale's *The Gentleman and Cabinet-Maker's Director* (first published in London in 1754) popularizing the exuberant new rococo style of highly-carved and figured surfaces, and serving as the foremost design guide for craftsmen and patrons.

Although several hundred cabinetmakers were working in the Boston area in the late 1700s, many of whom undoubtedly made block-front furniture, only seven block-front casepieces can be documented to a specific maker. Because so few chests were signed, and because cabinetmakers travelled constantly along the North Shore, training and working in various shops, it is impossible to establish with certainty where this chest was made.

—C.Z.

Figure 22.

CHEST-ON-CHEST, ca. 1800
Connecticut River Valley
Cherry, white pine
H: 77¼ in W: 40¼ in. D: 20 in.
Gift of Mrs. Gilbert Vaughn

This chest-on-chest is the work of a talented rural craftsman, and has endured for almost two centuries without brass pulls. Whether the original owner of the chest could not afford the decorative trimmings he desired is not known although they were imported from England and often expensive, sometimes costing more than the price of the casepiece itself. However, the wear marks at the sides of many of the drawers indicate clearly that the chest received much use over the years.

The chest-on-chest was a furniture form that became popular during the Chippendale period from the 1850s to 1880s. The classical simplicity of this casepiece with its flat rather than pedimented top, suggests that it was made around 1800. The graduated drawers, organization of the top drawers and the interlocking scribed design which borders the shell motif, together with the use of cherry as the primary wood, all suggest that the piece was made along the Connecticut River Valley, probably near Hartford.

—C.Z.

27

Fig. 22

Figure 23.
HIGH CHEST OF DRAWERS, 1789
Probably Asahel Jarvis, 1768–1823, Lanesborough, Massachusetts
Cherry, pine: finials are replacements
H: 81 in. W: 39½ in. D: 20 in.
Inscribed on the inside bottom of the third full drawer from the top: Made by Asahel Jarvis/of
Lanesborough/at Capt. Newal's Shop/LDP/Price L 6 0 0 0/February [?] 1789
Anonymous Gift

This high chest of drawers, made of cherry with a scalloped skirt, spiral rosettes, and a
sunburst on the top and bottom central drawers, together with the arrangement of the
drawers, resembles similar pieces made in Hartford or Wethersfield, Ct. in the late
18th century.

Made of thick boards and reinforced with joints which are both dove-tailed and
pegged, the chest is clearly the work of a versatile country cabinetmaker who
probably had few commissions to make case-pieces as sophisticated or expensive as
this one. The chest bears the inscription "Made by Asahel Jarvis/of Lanesborough/at

Fig. 23

Capt. Newal's Shop/LDP/Price L 6 0 0 0/February [?] 1789" and may well have been the production of Asahel Jarvis (1768–1823), a third generation descendant of Thomas Jarvis of the Norwalk area in Connecticut, who lived in Lanesborough, Mass. from at least 1780 until 1790. The "Capt. Newal" noted in the inscription may refer to Revolutionary War Captain Ebenezer Newell (1747–1808) who, at the time of his death, possessed many tools of the joiner's trade. However, no documentation has been found other than the inscription on this chest to suggest or substantiate that either Jarvis or Newell were cabinetmakers. Neither is known to have advertised in the local Berkshire County newspapers nor were they listed as craftsmen in the local census. In addition, no other furniture by them is known at this time. The "roll top" bonnet on this chest is very unusual and may be an alteration of the late 19th or early 20th century.

—C.Z.

Fig. 24

Figure 24.
CHEST OF DRAWERS, ca. 1815–1820
Attributed to George Stedman, b. 1795, of Chester, Norwich and possibly Shaftsbury, Vermont, and Jackson and Rome, New York
Cherry with mahogany and lightwood inlays, white pine
H: 36⅛ in. W: 41¾ in. D: 19¼ in.
Gift of Four Corners East

This elegant bow-front chest of drawers with flared French feet is one of eleven or twelve which have been attributed to George Stedman because of their resemblance to a chest in the Henry Francis du Pont Winterthur Museum collection which bears the pencilled inscription "Made by S.[G?] Stedman/Norwich/Vt."

Stedman was born in Chester, Vt. in 1795 where he probably apprenticed with cabinetmaker, Sampson Warner whose shop he later owned in 1816. Because many people from Connecticut settled in Vermont towns along the Connecticut River, there was a great deal of exchange between the upper and lower Connecticut Valley. Therefore, it is not surprising to find Stedman working in a manner indicative of the lower Connecticut Valley, using cherry instead of mahogany as a primary wood and mahogany and lightwood inlays.

However, it is curious that of all the furniture forms Stedman could have chosen to make he selected the sophisticated and complicated bow-front or bombe chest which could have been inspired by either French prototypes of the early 18th century or American interpretations of this form made in Boston and Salem between 1750 and 1800. In this rare example of a Federal Bombé form, the cabinetmaker has simplified and flattened the chest while at the same time giving it the stylish, decorative stringing and oval brasses more typical of the period.

—C.Z.

Fig. 25

Figure 25.
CHEST OF DRAWERS WITH CUPBOARDS, 1825.
Possibly "AHK" of Shaftsbury, Vermont
Mahogany and mahogany veneers, pine; glass pulls are replacements
H: 58½ in. W: 49¾ in. D: 23¼ in.
Pencilled notation on the bottom of the left top drawer:
No. 3/Shaftsbury/Oct. 7, 1825 AHK
Gift of Mr. and Mrs. Richard L. Hughes

This chest of drawers with cupboards and four locks was known as a "locker," and functioned as a sideboard for the storage of tablecloths, drinking glasses, dishes, bottles and silverware. According to family tradition, Judge John H. Olin of Shaftsbury had this chest made as a wedding present for his daughter Mary Ann, who married George Walbridge of Bennington on November 10, 1825. It remained in the Walbridge family until it was donated to the Museum in 1974.

Although the inscription "No. 3/Shaftsbury/Oct. 7, 1825 AHK" on the bottom of the top left drawer refers to the maker of this chest, no record exists for a maker with these initials in the *Vermont Gazette* in the 1820s. However, two cabinetmakers, (probably Jonathan) Howlett of Shaftsbury who advertised "elegant mahogany bureaus with drawers on top" for $22, and Jonathan Hastings Kendrick of Bennington, who offered a variety of casepieces and "All kinds of carvings done on short notice," had shops during this time period where the maker of this chest might have been employed.

The broken pediment, finely carved columns and hairy paw feet with acanthus leaves on this locker are similar to those found on Empire furniture made in Troy and Albany in the 1820s and 1830s, which is not surprising since there was extensive commercial activity between southern Vermont and eastern New York at this time.

Fig. 26

It is possible that the maker of this locker learned his craft in New York state or that the legs and feet for this chest were purchased from a New York City, Troy or Albany carver, since by this time, cabinetmaking had become quite specialized, and certain furniture parts were available separately. The mahogany used to make this chest and the brasses which originally adorned it, would have been brought into Shaftsbury, probably from New York as well.

The chest illustrates the heavy, deeply carved Empire style of furniture which was inspired by classical forms and popular in the United States from 1810 until 1850.

—C.Z.

Figure 26.
REDWARE, 19th c.
Probably eastern Massachusetts, and Maine, 19th Century
Lead-glazed earthenware
Mug H: 3⅞ in. W (w/handle): 3½ in.; Jar H: 8 in. D: 6 in.; Pitcher H: 10½ in. W (w/handle): 8½ in.; Jug H: 6¼ in. W (w/handle): 5¼ in.
Gifts of Mrs. William Whitman, Jr.

From 1650 to 1850, farmers who made pots during the long New England winters, and urban potters who often worked in small family-run shops year-round, made great quantities of redware in which to store, prepare and serve food. Made of local clays and wheel-thrown into simple forms, these pots were embellished with oxide glazes, colored slip (clay diluted in water) and/or impressed decoration. Often they were given a lead glaze coating as well, as seen on the objects illustrated here, which made them glossy and impervious to water.

There were hundreds of potters working in New England before 1800, many of them with potteries situated along the seacoast and other waterways, close to transportation and communication. In Massachusetts, Charlestown and South Danvers were the major ceramic centers and many potters, who later spread the craft to western Massachusetts and New Hampshire, trained in these cities. The mug, jar and pitcher shown here with brilliant oxide glazes were all thought to have come from eastern Massachusetts. The large pitcher, especially noteworthy for its green glaze, colored with copper oxide, was illustrated in the first color plate published by *The Magazine Antiques* in December, 1925. Although green highlights are occasionally found on New England redware, green pieces such as this are rare. The jug shown on the right is thought to have been made in Maine on the basis of its form and mottled yellow glaze.

The very survival of these pots is significant because they were made for common use and probably handled with much less care than more expensive, imported ceramics. Also, in part because they were very brittle and vulnerable to breakage, and because people realized as early as the late 1700s that the shiny lead glaze that made these pots waterproof also made them toxic, the manufacture of these common wares was phased out in the 19th century. Imported creamware plates and domestically produced stoneware crocks and jars replaced redware for everyday use in America.

—C.Z.

Figure 27.
JUG AND JAR, 1795–1800
Norton Pottery (1793–1894), Bennington, Vermont
Lead-glazed earthenware
H: 6 in. H: 9½ in.
Gifts of John Spargo

The redware jug and jar are the earliest known examples of pottery made in Bennington, Vermont. They come from the pottery of Captain John Norton, who moved to Bennington from Williamstown, Mass., in 1785 and set up a small pottery kiln on his farm in 1793. The jug was presented to local resident Omindia Gerry (1788–1880) sometime before 1796 by Abel Wadsworth, a potter who worked for Norton. In 1878 at the age of 90, Mrs. Gerry gave the jug to Bennington resident George Robinson who recorded its history at that time, and in 1922, it was acquired by John Spargo, first director of The Bennington Museum. The jar is an equally well-documented piece and was purchased by Sarah Ostrander before 1800 from the original Norton Pottery. After her death in 1828, the jar was passed down through the family for over 100 years before Spargo acquired it in the 1920s.

These pieces confirm the production of redware by John Norton before he shifted to the manufacture of stoneware in the early 19th century. Made of local clay, the jar is glazed in an "Albany slip," and decorated with a floral motif in yellow slip; the jar is covered with a lead glaze.

—K.N.

Fig. 27

Figure 28.
JUG, 1864
E. & L.P. Norton (1861–1881), Bennington, Vermont
Salt-glazed stoneware with cobalt decoration
H: 23½ in.
Impressed in rondel: CALVIN PARK/1864/MEMBER FROM WOODFORD; signed in cobalt: George J.
Bequest of Mrs. Elmer H. Johnson

Figure 29.
JUG, 1859
J. & E. Norton (1850–1859), or J. Norton & Co. (1859–1861), Bennington, Vermont
Salt-glazed stoneware with cobalt decoration
H: 26 in.
Impressed in rondel: LUMAN P. NORTON/12 GALLS./1859/IN VINO VERITAS
Gift of Isabel Cushman Leonard

Although a variety of containers for the storage of water, wine and other liquids were
in common production by the Norton Pottery in the 19th century, the great size of
these jugs and their elaborate decoration makes them particularly distinctive.

The vessel with the prancing stallion illustrated on the left, not a motif common
to Bennington, is one of two jugs that were presented to Calvin Park (1820–1864) of
Woodford, Vt. on the occasion of his election to the Vermont State Legislature. Park
was associated first in business and then marriage to Bennington's leading pottery

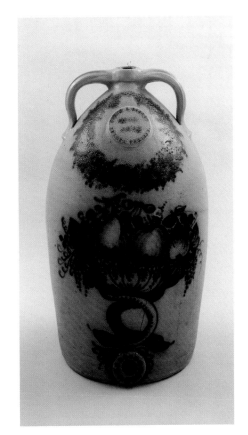

Fig. 28   Fig. 29

families. Between 1848 and 1849 he was a partner with Christopher Webber Fenton in the firm "Lyman, Fenton and Park" which sold dry goods and manufactured "Every Description of Rockingham, White Flint and White Earthen CROCKERY WARE." Ten years later in 1859, Park worked with Fenton again as manager of the A.A. Gilbert & Company, a short-lived reorganization of the United States Pottery. In 1864, the year Park received this jug, he was married to Christopher Webber Fenton's daughter, Fanny, the granddaughter of Judge Luman Norton, who helped to manage, or managed, the Norton pottery from 1812 until 1841. This piece of Bennington stoneware is of particular importance because it is one of very few signed examples. "George J.," whose name appears just below the horse, is thought to have decorated the jug.

The jug on the right, impressed with "IN VINO VERITAS," and painted decoration showing a wreath, basket of fruit and two tempting serpents, was given to Luman Preston Norton (1837–1906) in 1859, the year he joined the Norton Pottery.

—C.Z.

Fig. 30

Figure 30.
WATER COOLER, 1850–1859
J. & E. Norton (1850–1859), Bennington, Vermont
Salt-glazed stoneware with cobalt decoration
H: 33½ in.
Museum Purchase

Before the advent of electric refrigeration, stoneware vessels such as this one were filled with blocks of ice and water to dispense cool drinks on hot summer afternoons. This water cooler, which was used in the lobby of the Hotel Putnam in Bennington for many years, is one of the largest and most boldly decorated vessels ever made by the Norton Pottery.

From 1793 until 1894, for 101 years, the Norton family made and oversaw the production of high quality, utilitarian, salt-glazed stoneware in Bennington. Using clay brought up the Hudson River from Long Island and New Jersey, and transported in wagons to Bennington from Troy, the Nortons, made jugs, crocks, jars, bottles and water coolers on the potter's wheel for local use and distribution throughout New England and New York. Most of these vessels were painted with simple cobalt-blue floral motifs. However, occasionally they were painted with more elaborate and whimsical decoration. This water cooler, painted with three deer, fences, trees, a gabled house, pheasant, dog and blue bird, is virtually a design sampler of the motifs the pottery used at its height in the 1850s.

Although the decorator of this vessel remains unknown, it is very possibly the same person who painted similar encircling landscapes on a smaller, barrel-shaped cooler at The Bennington Museum and another, of almost equal size, at the Smithsonian Institution in Washington, D.C.

—C.Z.

Figure 31.
MONUMENT, 1851–1853
United States Pottery Company (1847–1858), Bennington, Vermont
Christopher Webber Fenton, 1806–1865, Designer; Modeler: Probably Daniel Greatbach (who worked in Bennington, Vt. from 1852–1858)
Bennington, Vermont
Earthenware, including scroddled ware, with Rockingham and flint enamel glazes and porcelain
H: 10 ft.
Bequest of Mrs. Henry D. Fillmore

In 1832, Christopher Webber Fenton (1806–1865), of an old family in Dorset, Vt., married Louisa Norton of Bennington's well-known pottery family. After several years of involvement with the pottery, Fenton entered a brief partnership with his wife's brother, Julius in 1844 or 1845, manufacturing "Every Description of STONE WARE." While Julius Norton was dedicated to producing the more traditional, wheel-thrown, utilitarian, salt-glazed crockery that his family was famous for, Fenton was eager to mold the more ornamental glazed forms of yellowware. These ceramics had become popular in England and the United States, and were already being manufactured by potteries in South Amboy and Jersey City, N.J.

In 1847, Fenton broke off from Julius Norton and began producing, independently, Rockingham and flint enameled ceramics together with "white flint ware, earthen, and china." The United States Pottery Company, incorporated in 1853, was modeled after the huge yellowware manufacturers in England, whose products the

Fig. 31

company imitated. The Pottery became the largest and most successful yellowware producer in New England, and by 1858, employed over 150 workers.

In 1853, Fenton had an opportunity to exhibit his ceramics at the Crystal Palace Exhibition held in New York City, America's first world's fair. In a dramatic display, Fenton advertised the diversity of both utilitarian and ornamental wares produced by the pottery. The Monument illustrated here was the focal point of Fenton's exhibit and is made in four sections, illustrating a variety of clays and glazes: the base was of scroddled ware, or mixed clays, resembling variegated marble; the second section was of yellowware showing Fenton's famous flint enamel glaze; the third section featured a parian bust of Fenton (not shown in this photograph) surrounded by corinthian columns of scroddled ware with a flint enamel glaze. Finally, the monument was crowned with a parian statue of a woman draped in robes, who held a bible toward the child in her arms.

Fenton's display received rave reviews. Horace Greeley of the *New York Tribune* stated, "In the United States Department is an exhibition which is well worth the observation by all who delight in the progress of American art and skill . . ." and *Gleason's Pictorial* (published in Boston) featured the Pottery's display with a front page article and full page illustration. The favorable publicity drawn by the exhibit prompted many orders followed by a short-lived period of prosperity and expansion. However, by 1855, Fenton was in financial trouble and although the Pottery had an established reputation and more orders than it could produce, it was forced to close its doors in 1858.

Following the exhibition, the monument stood for over 100 years on the porch of a double-house owned by Judge Luman Norton and his son-in-law, Christopher Webber Fenton. In 1897, the Pennsylvania Museum and School of Industrial Art, (known for its fine American pottery collection) attempted to acquire the monument. However, they were unsuccessful and the monument remained in Bennington. In 1968, it was given to the Museum where it is an impressive reminder of the United States Pottery's commanding position in the ceramic industry during the 19th century.

—C.Z.

Figure 32.
MANTEL FIGURES, 1847–1858
United States Pottery Company (1847–1858), Bennington, Vermont
Yellowware with Rockingham and flint enamel glazes

PAIR OF DOGS WITH BASKETS
Unmarked
H: 8½ in. W: 9½ in. D: 4 in.
Gift of the Estate of Ruth Hart Eddy and Museum Purchase

STANDING LION ON BASE
Impressed: Lyman Fenton & Co./Fenton's ENAMEL PATENTED. 1849/BENNINGTON, Vt. in circle
H: 9¼ in. W: 11 in. D: 6 in.
Bequest of Mrs. Elmer H. Johnson

RECUMBENT COW ON BASE
Impressed: Lyman Fenton & Co./Fenton's ENAMEL PATENTED. 1849/BENNINGTON, Vt. in circle
H: 5¾ in. W: 10¼ in. D: 5½ in.
Bequest of Mrs. Elmer H. Johnson

RECUMBENT DEER ON BASE
Impressed: Lyman Fenton & Co./Fenton's ENAMEL PATENTED, 1849/BENNINGTON, Vt. in circle
H: 10⅛ in. W: 11¹³⁄₁₆ in. D: 5¾ in.
Gift of Mrs. Elmer H. Johnson

Fig. 32

The American demand for English ceramic mantel figures in the early 1800s led to their wide manufacture in this country from 1840 to 1870. Potteries making yellow-ware in Bennington, Vt.; East Liverpool, Oh.; and South Amboy, Woodbridge and Trenton, N. J. all produced these chimney ornaments as well as novelty items such as cow creamers, toby jugs, snuff jars and bottles, banks and bookcases to satisfy the Victorian penchant for artistic objects to decorate their parlors.

It is not surprising that the United States Pottery's animal figures look very much like English ones as an Englishman, Daniel Greatbach, was recruited to be chief modeler at the Pottery in 1852 and designed many of them, drawing his inspiration from English prototypes. The United States Pottery's standing lion with paw on ball closely resembles a lion produced by Thomas Whieldon at his factory in England in the 1760s, while similarly the recumbent stag is said to resemble a design by Ralph Wood, a contemporary of Whieldon in England. The cow illustrated here with a spillholder, (to hold small slivers of wood used for lighting lamps) is also based on English examples in porcelain or other white earthenware, and the Pottery's standing poodles with baskets and cole slaw manes are inspired by similar English Staffordshire figurines of this favorite household pet. The poodles were made in many variations with and without mustaches, top-knots, eyebrows or tufts on the legs. All of these figures except for the cows, are thought to have been made in pairs.

—C.Z.

Fig. 33

Figure 33.
STANDING STAG, ca. 1852
Daniel Greatbach, 1852–1858
United States Pottery Company (1847–1858),
Bennington, Vermont
Yellowware with Rockingham glaze; base and
stump: yellowware with flint enamel glaze
H: 14 in. W: 9⅝ in. D: 5¼ in.
Bequest of Mrs. Elmer H. Johnson, (ex-collection
of Charles H. Tyler)

This piece is the only known example of the standing stag produced by the United States Pottery in Bennington, and was included in the Pottery's display at the 1853 Crystal Palace Exhibition held in New York. The stag was modeled by Daniel Greatbach, who had come to Bennington from England the previous year to serve as chief designer and modeler at the pottery.

It is thought that the standing stag, because of its slender, long legs, was probably considered too delicate for production, even with the stump support, and as a result was adapted to a reclining position. (see. p. 39)

—C.Z.

Figure 34.
"CASCADE" PITCHER, 1854
United States Pottery Company (1847–1858), Bennington, Vermont
Painted highly glazed white porcelain
H: 9⅟₁₆ in. W (with handle): 8⅜ in. D: 6¼ in.
Marked: on bottom in black paint: U.S. Pottery./Bennington, Vt./1854
Gift of Robert B. and Marie P. Condon

"SAINT NICHOLAS" or "SWEETHEART" PITCHER, ca. 1855
United States Pottery Company (1847–1858), Bennington, Vermont
Graniteware painted in gold and colors
H: 6¼ in. W (with handle): 8 in. D: 5 in.
Marked: painted on side: United States Pottery Co./Bennington, Vt. and reverse:
Samuel H. Johnson/76 Pearl St., New York,
Museum Collection

The United States Pottery made a variety of earthenware and porcelain forms which were both functional and decorative. As is the case with most American ceramics made in the 19th century, the majority of these objects were never stamped with the mark of the pottery possibly because they were standard, commercial items or so they would not be identified as American. Although the United States Pottery had a reputation for making high quality wares, American consumers generally preferred English and European to domestically produced ceramics at that time. These two pitchers are exceptional because they are painted with inscriptions which identify them as the production of the United States Pottery of Bennington, Vt.

The "Cascade" Pitcher on the left, one of few designs unique to the United States Pottery, was inspired by the rocks and rushing waters of Niagara Falls, one of America's great natural wonders and a popular tourist attraction in the 19th century.

Fig. 34

Although the pitcher does not appear in illustrations of the Pottery's display at the Crystal Palace Exhibition in New York in 1853, a contemporary description of the objects shown there refers to "a large water pitcher intended to represent a waterfall with rocks in front and water overflowing the mouth and falling in volumes down the sides in relief."

This pitcher is one of few known examples of painted porcelain made at the United States Pottery, and might have been painted by Theophile Frey who worked at the Sevres Porcelain Works in Sevres, France before coming to Bennington. Frey worked at the Pottery from 1849 to 1858 where he was best known for his decoration of graniteware "sweetheart pitchers," such as the one shown on the right.

Between 1840 and 1890 "sweetheart" or "St. Nicholas" pitchers were manufactured by American potteries from New York to Ohio. Although many of these were painted with the name of the person to whom they were presented, few are inscribed with the name of the "United States Pottery." The one pictured here is of particular importance as it was a gift to Samuel H. Johnson who helped to reincorporate the Pottery in 1855, and who served as an agent for the company in New York City through 1858.

—C.Z.

Figure 35.
FOUR PITCHERS
United States Pottery Company 1847–1858, Bennington, Vermont
Porcelain and Parian Ware
H: 9⅛ in.; 9⅞ in.; 7⅛ in.; 8¼ in.
Museum Purchase; Anonymous gifts, and Gift of Mrs. E. H. Johnson

These four pitchers are excellent examples of the United States Pottery's production and its diversity. They all bear the ribbon mark of the pottery which was used primarily on Parian, and blue and white porcelain. The brown and white syrup pitcher is extremely rare and unusual because of its color, and carries a raised ribbon

Fig. 35

mark numbered "10." The blue and white "Paul and Virginia" pitcher also bears "10" on its ribbon mark and illustrates with Victorian sentimentality the story of a shipwreck on an island. The lily pattern pitcher exhibits another favorite motif of this period which is often found illustrated in Victorian Day books in many different media. Likewise the charter oak pattern was also widely used for decoration and, according to tradition, received its name as a result of the Connecticut Charter, which was in danger of being taken by the King's men, having been hidden in an oak tree and saved.

Porcelain, first made in China A.D. 618–907, was introduced to the west through early explorers. Difficult and expensive to produce, the first attempts to manufacture it in America were unsuccessful. In addition, the market was limited, since those who could pay the price preferred the more stylish pieces, imported from England or the Continent. Parian, a type of porcelain having the appearance of marble, was first made in America in the mid-1840s at the pottery of Christopher Webber Fenton and his brother-in-law Julius Norton (the son of the founder of the Norton pottery). With the aid of English craftsmen they broke away from the old stoneware tradition, and by the 1850s Fenton was producing porcelain in Bennington which included some of the finest made in America at the time. When, in 1853, Fenton's pottery was impressively displayed at the Crystal Palace Exhibition in New York City, Horace Greeley of the *New York Tribune* noted: "The Parian ware of this Company is remarkably fine, especially in the form of pitchers. They are light in material, of graceful outline . . ."

The unglazed Parian with the color and texture of unpolished marble could be cast to achieve an unusually high degree of detail and was far less expensive than marble. Eagerly recognizing this, the pottery at Bennington produced a wide variety of pieces that graced many American parlors.

—R.L.

Fig. 36

Figure 36.
HOUND HANDLED PITCHER,
ca. 1853
United States Pottery Company (1847–1858),
Bennington, Vermont
Daniel Greatbach
Scroddledware (variegated earthenware)
H: 11⅛ in.
Gift of Mrs. George Van Santvoord

The Bennington hound handled pitcher was designed by Daniel Greatbach, grandson of William Greatbach an associate of the well-known Wedgwood Pottery in England. Daniel arrived in America about 1839, became chief designer and modeler for the American Pottery Manufacturing Company in Jersey City, N.J. and, while there, designed a hound handled pitcher, possibly the first in America. By 1852 Greatbach was a resident of Bennington and chief designer for the United States Pottery Co. where he designed a second hound handled pitcher. Greatbach worked at the U.S. Pottery until 1858 at which time he left to establish another pottery in Kaolin, Ga. with Christopher Webber Fenton and Decius Clark.

The hound or dog handled pitcher was made in large numbers by the United States Pottery Co. and after it closed was produced by the E. and L.P. Norton Pottery in four sizes until at least 1867. While no longer common, these pitchers are in many public and private collections and can be found in antique shops today. The dog, as modeled by Daniel Greatbach, has a chain collar, a sharp keel-like shape on the underside, and stylized hind quarters which form the lower part of the handle. In addition, the dog's nose usually touches the forepaws which grasp the rim, and prominent ribs can be felt, if not seen, under the glaze. No other hound pitcher made by other firms, and there are many, is identical to the Bennington hound. The chain collar is a particularly important characteristic for identification.

Scroddled ware has always been the scarcest ware produced by the United States Pottery. Wedging or combining two colors of clay together, then pressing it into molds, created a veining effect which, as a result, permeated the entire piece. Scroddled ware was therefore not only time consuming and expensive but also difficult to make into sets which were well matched. In addition, when used for figural pieces such as toby pitchers, the facial features became lost among the veining.

The hound handled pitcher shown here is the only one known in scroddled ware and the ice strainer over the spout is a rare detail on any Bennington pitcher, making this piece a doubly desirable one.

—E.K.

Fig. 37

Figure 37.
PAIR OF BLUE DECANTERS, 1825–1835
Attributed to Boston & Sandwich Glass Co. (1825–1888), Sandwich, Massachusetts
Cobalt-colored lead glass; stoppers not original
H (w/stopper): 10¾ in.
Channing Hare-Mountford Coolidge Collection

Although wealthy Americans used cut and engraved decanters imported from England and Ireland as early as 1750, these forms were not available to the middle class
until the 1820s, when the Roman technique of blown molded glass was revived and
these forms were produced in large quantities. Most of these blown-molded decanters
were made of clear lead glass; this pair is distinctive for its brilliant cobalt-blue
coloring.

 The first patterns for blown-molded glass were geometric and imitated cut glass
designs. Subsequent patterns included more flowing lines and curvilinear motifs
which exploited the plasticity of glass and demonstrated the glassworker's liberation
from the rigid designs dictated by the cutter's wheel. Motifs such as bands of beading,
stars, hearts, palmettes and the "shell and rib" design shown here, were common to
later blown-molded glass. By the 1830s, blown molded glass was superseded by the
more efficient technology of pressed glass, and decanters such as these became
obsolete.

 These decanters have been attributed to the Boston & Sandwich Glass Company
because fragments of the same pattern have been found on the factory site.

—C.Z.

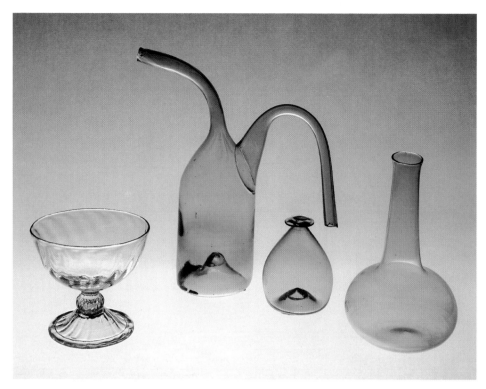

Fig. 38

Figure 38.
VERMONT GLASS
The Vermont Glass Factory (1810–1817), and The Lake Dunmore Glass Company (1832–1842),
Salisbury, Vermont
Green glass (common bottle glass)
Chemical glassware H: 9 in.; Ribbed compote H: 3⅝ in.; Half of an hour glass H: 3¼ in.; Laboratory
flask H: 6⅝ in.
Museum purchase from the Estate of Mrs. Gertrude D. Webster, Gift of Mr. & Mrs. Stanley B. Ineson

Although the first glass furnaces were built in Jamestown, Va. in 1607, glass was not
manufactured on a large scale in this country until the War of 1812, when restrictions
on English imports prompted the development of American window, bottle, and
flint-glass tableware manufacture. The Vermont Glass Factory, founded in Salisbury,
Vt. in 1810, was one of more than 40 glasshouses established in America between 1808
and 1814.

The Vermont Glass Factory, with a State charter granting it a monopoly in glass
production for 12 years and exemption from taxes, appeared destined for success. By
1810, there was a growing demand for window glass and bottles, in particular, as
Vermont grew rapidly and the natural resources essential for glass production were
close at hand. Situated on the shores of Lake Dunmore in Salisbury, the Vermont Glass
Factory was surrounded by sand, a major ingredient of glass, as well as by wood used
for fueling the furnaces. This company, which made window glass, had easy access to
a market as it was located near the main highway in western Vermont where freight
wagons provided transportation to Middlebury, Rutland, and Windsor. The *Literary
and Philosophical Repertory* in Middlebury noted in 1813: "Should the glass produced at

Fig. 39

the [Vermont Glass] factory prove as good as it now promises to be, the inhabitants of Vermont will derive incalculable benefits from the establishment." Because the future of the glassworks looked so promising, a branch glasshouse specializing in the production of various articles, including bottles, opened in East Middlebury soon after 1813. However, as fate would have it, the Vermont Glass Factory soon failed. Severe financial problems and a fire at the window glassworks in 1815 forced the branch factory to close in 1816, and the window glassworks to close in 1817.

In 1832 the factory reopened as the Lake Dunmore Glass Company. Little is known about this enterprise except that it made window glass until approximately 1841. The only other glasshouse known to have operated in Vermont was the Lake Champlain Glass Company, located in Burlington, which made window glass and possibly bottles from 1847 until 1850.

Of particular interest is the laboratory glass illustrated here which is thought to have been custom-made for the chemistry department of Middlebury College where Henry R. Schoolcraft, superintendant of the Vermont Glass Factory from 1813 to 1815, was a student.

—C.Z.

Figure 39.
LILY-PAD BOWL, 1830–1850
Redwood Glassworks (1832–1852), near Watertown, New York, or Redford Crown Glassworks (1832–1877), near Plattsburg, New York
H: 14⅛ in.
Green glass (common bottle glass)
Gift of Joseph and May Limric

Because of its aqua color, lily-pad decoration, and superior craftsmanship, this extraordinary large bowl of common bottle glass is thought to have been made either at the Redwood or Redford Crown Glassworks in upstate New York, makers of the most brilliantly- colored and finely-crafted glass lily-pad bowls, pitchers, plates, creamers and sugar bowls made in the mid-19th century.

Since Roman times, free-blown glass has been embellished by cutting, engrav-

Fig. 40

ing, and crimping the glass, by coloring it, and by applying threading and chains to its surface. The lily-pad decoration on this bowl was achieved by partially covering a blown glass form with a second gather of glass which was then pulled to achieve this design, a decorative technique used in northern Europe in the 1700s and practiced regularly in American glasshouses, especially in New Jersey and New York between 1830 and 1870.

By the 1830s, there were primarily three different types of glass factories in America: those which made windows and bottles; pressed glass, or fine flint glass tableware. This bowl and other free-blown objects confirm that blown glass continued to be appreciated in the 19th century despite the growing popularity of standardized pressed glass forms which were being produced in great quantity at this time. Current scholarship suggests that these free-blown forms of bottle glass were made as special pieces and sold by glasshouses in limited quantities.

—C.Z.

Figure 40.
VASE, ca. 1886
Albert Steffin
Mount Washington Glass Works (1869–1957),
New Bedford, Massachusetts
Burmese Glass
H: 17½ in.
Painted on base: A. Steffin
Gift of Mr. and Mrs. Joseph Limric

In the 1870s and 1880s, American glass manufacturers experimented with numerous formulas to satisfy a tremendous new demand for colorful glassware decorated in exotic styles. Burmese glass, patented by Frederick Shirley of the Mount Washington Glass Company in 1885, was one of the most popular and attractive of these new wares. It shades from a delicate salmon pink to pastel yellow, and the softness of the colors is further enhanced by the acid finish given to the glass before the application of enamelled ornamentation.

Fig. 41

The Egyptian-style vase at The Bennington Museum is among the most spectacular pieces of Burmese glass known to exist. One of four or five surviving examples signed by the superintendent of the decorating department, Albert Steffin, it appears to be associated with the famous Burmese tea set presented to Queen Victoria in 1886. This set, which has since disappeared, inspired the firm of Thomas Webb and Sons to purchase Shirley's patent rights for the production of Burmese in England. It was described at length by the *New Bedford Evening Standard* in November of 1886. The set included "four vases, two of Egyptian and two of Etruscan pattern," and the reporter took care to note that "everything in the ornamentation is of original design by Mr. Albert Steffin."

—K.N.

Figure 41.
PLATED AMBERINA GROUP, ca. 1886
The New England Glass Company (1818–1888), Cambridge, Massachusetts
Pitcher H: 7½ in.; Cruet H: 6¾ in.; Tumber H 3¾ in.; Punch Cup H: 2½ in.
Gift of Mr. and Mrs. Joseph Limric

Plated amberina glass was made for a limited time beginning in 1886 exclusively by the New England Glass Company of Cambridge, Mass. Established in 1818, the company proved to be prosperous and long-lived, operating until 1888 when it relocated to Toledo, Oh. under the name of the Libbey Glass Company. For many years, the New England Glass Company excelled in the production of fine cut and engraved lead glass.

During the last decades of the 19th century, the emphasis on beautifying one's home created a demand for fanciful and exotic objects. Glass manufacturers responded with a succession of "novelty" wares, glass in an astonishing array of new and unusual colors and forms. The New England Glass Company contributed a number of innovative and popular glasswares, many of which were inspired or created by their head designer, John Locke.

John Locke (1846–1936) established his reputation as a glassmaker in England. In 1882, Locke came to Boston where he was employed immediately by the New England Glass Company and in the following year he patented amberina glass, one of the first tinted glasses. Traditionally, the origin of amberina has been attributed to a workman's wedding band that accidently slipped into a batch of amber glass. After a mixture of amber glass containing a precise amount of gold was blown, any portions reheated turned a rich ruby red, while the unheated glass remained a delicate amber. Amberina was soon one of the company's most successful lines, which prompted their competitors to market their own versions, such as the Mount Washington Glass Company's "Rose Amber."

In 1886 Locke patented plated amberina, which had the same shading as amberina but was lined with milk-white glass. To achieve this effect, a quantity of opalescent glass was gathered onto the end of the glassmaker's blowpipe which, in turn, was covered with amberina glass, and the two were blown together to form two cohesive layers. The glass was then blown into a mold to produce the ribbing characteristic of all plated amberina. Final shaping was done by hand after which handles were applied separately.

Plated amberina was ultimately an unsuccessful venture since the two layers had different rates of expansion and as a result had a tendency to crack while cooling. Consequently, only a small amount was made and few pieces have survived. Other forms of plated amberina included creamers, toothpick holders, syrup pitchers, salt and pepper shakers and bowls. While the Libbey Glass Company revived the manufacture of amberina in 1917, plated amberina was never produced again.

—L.J.G.

Figure 42.
VASE, ca. 1905
Tiffany Furnaces (1893–1920), Corona, New York
Favrile glass
H: 5⅛ in.
Incised on base: L.C.T. Y 2290
Gift of Mr. and Mrs. Joseph Limric

Louis Comfort Tiffany (1848–1933), was the son of Charles L. Tiffany, founder of Tiffany & Company, the internationally renowned jeweler of New York. As a young man Tiffany had been trained as a painter, and in 1876 he exhibited several pictures at the Philadelphia Centennial Exposition. There he was inspired, as were many others by the decorative arts of exotic cultures which had captured his attention in years previous during travels abroad. In 1879, he joined with Candace Wheeler, Lockwood de Forest, and Samuel Colman to form an interior decorating company called the Associated Artists. This group provided custom textiles, woodwork, tiles and stained glass for the homes of some of the wealthiest men of the day. Tiffany, who created the stained glass windows for these commisssions, organized his own business in 1885, Tiffany Glass Company, to produce windows independently, and to continue his experiments with glass.

At the 1893 Columbian Exposition in Chicago, Tiffany exhibited a chapel of mosaics and stained glass, for which he earned 54 medals and international recognition. Among his admirers was the prominent Parisian art dealer, S. Bing, a champion

Fig. 42

of the Art Nouveau style, who began selling Tiffany's works in his gallery. That same year, Tiffany began the production of Favrile glassware, a line of artistic vases and decorative tablewares which, while still expensive, were available to a wider audience. In 1899, he started making the leaded glass lamps for which he is now famous.

Tiffany's innovative creations found a ready market in America, where the popularity of art glass such as Amberina and Peachblow had begun in the 1870s. Tiffany aspired to provide superior, and even enlightening, objects for the home in his belief that "it is all a matter of education and we shall never have good art in our homes until the people learn to distinguish the beautiful from the ugly."

Tiffany's long-time fascination with ancient glass led him to develop glass that replicated its textures and iridescent qualities. This iridescent vase is one of thousands of objects blown at the Tiffany Furnaces. The term "favrile," derived from the Old English word for hand-made, was registered as a Tiffany trademark in 1894, and was described as:

> "a hand-made glass or vitrified body invented and used more particularly for the making of colored or stained glass windows, mosaics, glassware, etc. . . . It may therefore be either flat, foliated, convoluted, cylindrical, globular or cubical, of one color or many, laminated, floriated or foliatious."

This outstanding example of Favrile glass is decorated with millefiori (Italian for a thousand flowers), thin discs of colored glass that were applied to the surface of the blown object, which was then rolled on a flat surface until the designs were completely embedded. Threads of colored glass were then pulled across the surface to create tendrils, after which the glass was subjected to tin-chloride fumes to achieve what the company called a "diversified radiance of iridescence." Other types of favrile glass included laminated glass, which resembled agate; Cypriote glass, which had the pitted surface of ancient glass; lava glass, which simulated volcanic rock; and glass in flower forms, which, perhaps, were among the most beautiful of Tiffany's many stunning creations.

—L.J.G.

Fig. 43

Figure 43.

TRAY, 1830–1840
Probably Boston & Sandwich Glass Company (1825–1888), Sandwich, Massachusetts
Lead glass
L: 11¼ in.
Channing Hare-Mountford Coolidge Collection by Exchange
CREAMER, 1829–1832
R.B. Curling & Sons (1829–1832), Pittsburgh, Pa.
Lead glass
H: 4 in.
Channing Hare-Mountford Coolidge Collection by Exchange

This tray and creamer are extremely rare and successful early examples of pressed glass. The first products of this new technology, developed in America in the 1820s, were regularly given a strippled background to distract viewers from flaws in pressing such as bubbles, folds or varying thicknesses in the glass. These elaborately impressed pieces are known as "lacy glass."

The tray pictured on the left was a particularly difficult design to execute because it required forcing molten glass to flow and fill the chain-border and handle before cooling, a process which was slowed by the highly modeled background. The incomplete handle on the left of the tray illustrates a problem that resulted from molding such an intricate form. This is an early, and perhaps first, version of the tray design which was modified to expedite the flow of the glass into the mold. In a later version, the stippling on the top and bottom of the chain border was removed as were the stars between the border links and leaf scrolls on each side of the tray. Very few examples of either state of this tray are known today as only small quantities of this challenging and intricate design were made. The tray is attributed to the Boston & Sandwich Glass Company because fragments of this piece have been found at the factory site.

The creamer on the left is one of only two known examples of this form (the second is at the Corning Museum of Glass) and one of very few pieces of molded glass bearing the name of the company which made it. The bottom of the creamer is impressed "R.B. CURLING & SONS FORT PITT," and was probably marked to distinguish it from the production of the Boston & Sandwich Glass Company, one of the leading producers of lacy pressed glass. Until the discovery of this creamer in the early 1930s, it was thought that all lacy glass came from Sandwich. However, this creamer is proof that New England did not have a monopoly on the production of lacy glassware. In fact, a number of factories were producing pressed glass in Pittsburgh in the 1820s and 1830s. Among these companies were: Bakewell, Page & Bakewell, J. Robinson & Son, and Curling & Price, which later became R.B. Curling & Sons in 1829. Because of their proximity to both coal and natural gas, western Pennsylvania and Ohio became the major centers for pressed glass production in the late 19th century.

—C.Z.

Figure 44.
BLOWN-MOLDED CANDLESTICK AND DECANTER STOPPER,
1820–1840
Attributed to the Boston and Sandwich Glass Company (1825–1888), Sandwich, Massachusetts
Clear lead glass
H: 5⅛ in.; H: 3⅝ in.
Gift of Mrs. William Whitman, Jr.

This candlestick of blown, three-mold glass is the only one of its kind known today. Made from an inverted decanter stopper placed on the foot of a wine glass, the candlestick illustrates how the glassblower could manipulate the glass on the pontil rod after it had been blown into a patterned wooden or metal mold to create a variety of forms.

Over 150 different blown, three-mold patterns have been identified on American glass, including geometric, baroque and arch designs. The geometric designs were among the earliest used and appear commonly on decanters, bottles, carafes, drinking vessels, plates, bowls, pitchers and many other forms, all of which are represented in The Bennington Museum's collection.

Blown-molded glass is known to have been made at glass factories in Kent and Mantua, Oh.; Vernon, N.Y.; Coventry, Ct.; Keene, NH., and Sandwich and East Cambridge, Mass. from the early 1820s until the mid-1830s when it was replaced by the more efficient production of pressed glass. Since these molded pieces are rarely marked, and because the mold designers and glass workers frequently moved from one glass factory to another taking their designs with them, it is virtually impossible to know where glass was manufactured without a definite and complete history of ownership. In this case, because fragments

Fig. 44

Fig. 45

of glass with the same pattern have been found on the factory site, it is possible to attribute the candlestick and decanter stopper to the Boston & Sandwich Glass Company.

—C.Z.

Figures 45 and 46.
EPERGNE, ca. 1876, and PAIR OF PAPERWEIGHT VASES, 1870–1880
Nicholas Lutz, 1835–1904
Boston & Sandwich Glass Company (1825–1888)
Milk-white glass with red and white loopings; lead glass
Epergne H: 19¼ in.; vases H: 7⅛ in., 7¼ in.
Gift of Mr. and Mrs. Ferdinand L. Meyer, (ex-collection of Victor Lutz); Gift of Joseph and May Limric, (ex-collection of Victor Lutz)

Nicholas Lutz, the maker of this colorful looped glass epergne and pair of paper-weight vases was a master craftsman, specializing in the creation of elaborately colored, striped or "Venetian" and "looped" glass and paperweights, at the Boston & Sandwich Glass Company.

Fig. 46

This red, white and blue epergne, colored to celebrate America's Centennial, and these vases, were made as gifts for Lutz's wife, Elizabeth, and were once owned by Lutz's son, Victor. As such, they are significant not only for their aesthetic appeal, but also for their positive attribution to this celebrated glassblower.

A native of Alsace, France, Lutz apprenticed for seven years at the Cristalleries de St. Louis, famous for the production of paperweights, before moving to America in 1860 to work for the distinguished Alsatian, Christian Dorflinger, founder of the Greenpoint Glassworks in Brooklyn, N. Y. and the Wayne County Glassworks in White Mills, Penn. Lutz worked with Dorflinger making paperweights, among other objects, until 1867 when he moved to Massachusetts to work for the New England Glass Company and later the Boston & Sandwich Glass Company from 1869 until it closed in 1888.

Although Lutz was not the first to make paperweights at Sandwich, his paperweights of flowers and small free-blown fruits and vegetables, as seen in the two examples illustrated here, are considered to be some of the finest produced at the Sandwich Factory. Numerous other objects made by or under the direction of Nicholas Lutz are in The Bennington Museum collection including poinsettias, assorted leaves and fruits which Lutz used in his paperweights, glass pens once owned by Victor Lutz, and a variety of threaded glassware.

—C.Z.

Fig. 47

Figure 47.
OPEN-WORK COMPOTE, 1840s–1870s
Attributed to: Boston & Sandwich Glass Company (1825–1888), Sandwich, Massachusetts
Amethyst-colored lead glass
H: 8 in.
Channing Hare-Mountford Coolidge Collection

One of a pair, this glass open-work compote, inspired by contemporary ceramic prototypes, is a stellar example of panelled, pressed glass produced in the mid-19th century. Both its form, a particularly difficult design to produce because of the ribbed-nature of the bowl, and the compote's brilliant amethyst coloring (achieved with manganese oxide) make it distinctive.

Pressed glass was an American innovation of the 1820s which revolutionized the glass industry, transferred the artistry of glassmaking from the domain of the glass-blower to the mold-maker, and made glass affordable to the middle class for the first time. The earliest known patents for mass producing forms by forcing molten glass into wooden or metal molds with a plunger date from between 1825 and 1830 for the production of furniture knobs, salt dishes and cup plates. These objects were usually given a stippled background to hide any flaws in pressing such as bubbles, uneven thicknesses and wrinkles. As methods of manufacture were perfected, glass factories graduated to making simpler panelled forms, which drew attention to the clean pressed surfaces.

This compote, an example of later pressed glass, was probably made at the Boston & Sandwich Glass Company (1825–1888) of Sandwich, Mass. This company and the New England Glass Company (1818–1888) of East Cambridge, Mass., were the first to manufacture pressed glass commercially on a large scale. In 1839, the Boston & Sandwich Glass Company covered a six acre site and employed 225 workers; 31 years later, over 600 men and boys worked in this plant, one of the largest

Fig. 48

in operation at this time in New England. The neighboring New England Glass Company was close in size, produced comparable tablewares, and often employed the same workers.

The Metropolitan Museum of Art in New York and the Sandwich Glass Museum in Sandwich, Mass., each have single amethyst colored, open-work compotes in their collections.

—C.Z.

Figure 48.
PAIR OF VASES, 1840–1860
Boston & Sandwich Glass Company (1825–1888), Sandwich, Massachusetts
Emerald green-colored lead glass
H: 12¼ in. and 12 in.
Miss Dorothy Lee-Jones and Channing Hare-Mountford Coolidge Collection

Many consider these monument-based vases to be the finest pressed glass forms produced by the Boston & Sandwich Glass Company between 1840 and 1860. The vases were molded in two parts, as pressed vases, lamps and candlesticks commonly were, and then joined with either one or two wafers of molten glass.

By molding the bases and tops separately, glass manufacturers were able to produce a variety of composite forms occasionally using two different colors. After being molded, the upper portion of the form could then be tooled open to make a vase or closed to make a lamp font increasing the design options for the manufacturer. The classical bases seen here usually supported closed fonts rather than open vase forms.

Like most large glass houses, Sandwich had a mold-making department where designers worked on the development of new forms and patterns. Since these designers regularly moved from factory to factory it is not surprising that the products of the various glass houses are similar in appearance. In addition, independent mold-makers

Fig. 49

in Boston, Philadelphia and Pittsburgh also provided smaller glass factories with stock molds making the identification of the production of glass to a particular factory even more difficult. The vases shown here are thought to be made by the Boston & Sandwich Glass Company on the basis of related documented forms. Another pair of emerald colored vases is in the collection of the Henry Ford Museum in Dearborn, Michigan. A clear vase of the same form and design, without surface cutting, is in the Sandwich Glass Museum in Sandwich, Massachusetts.

—C.Z.

Figure 49.
SAMPLER QUILT, 1863
Jane A. Stickle, 1817–1896
Shaftsbury, Vermont
Cotton
H: 80¼ in. W: 80¼ in.
Sewn inscription l.r. In War Time 1863/Pieces 5602/Jane A. Stickle
Museum Purchase

This sampler of heroic proportions has an unusual pieced and scalloped border, and is made up of 169 five-inch blocks, each differing in pattern, containing a total of 5,602 pieces. Although little is known of the maker, Jane A. Stickle, her burial is noted in records of the Center Shaftsbury Cemetery. From the 1863 date of the quilt, we know it was made during the Civil War, and Jane Stickle was 46 years old when it was completed.

Quilting first originated in Europe but quickly became popular during the Colonial period and represents a craft technique that has remained virtually unchanged over time. Although there is great variety in the actual surface decoration, the construction of most quilts is the same and essentially involves stitching together two layers of material, cut to size, usually with a filler in between the layers to provide extra warmth.

Patchwork quilts are among the most decorative and picturesque quilts that were made during the 19th century in America. They represent not only the artistic expression of the women who made them but also their delight in color, their skill at needlework and the pride they took in mastering the intricacies as well as the difficulty of the craft. The extraordinary variety found in this quilt makes it of particular importance as does its documentation to a specific event and time in history.

—R.L.

Fig. 50

Figure 50.
DRESS UNIFORM, 1803
Wool and lace
Gift of Jarvis Cromwell

When William Jarvis was a young merchant in Boston, he was appointed in 1801 by President Jefferson to be charge d'affairs and consul to Lisbon, Portugal where he subsequently took up residence. Shortly after his arrival, in 1803, a prince was born to the royal household in Portugal and Consul Jarvis, together with other high-ranking officials, was invited to celebrate the event. After much consideration, Jarvis ordered an American naval uniform of exquisite taste and embroidery, complete with large, gilt buttons decorated with the American eagle, to be specially made for the occasion by Carter's of London.

Jarvis returned to the United States with his family in 1810 bringing with him a herd of Merino sheep, the pride of Spain where they had been raised exclusively for centuries and for which strong penalties existed for exporting them. Two years later in 1812, Jarvis purchased almost the entire village of Weathersfield, Vt. where he continued to raise sheep for several years. As a result of Jarvis' efforts, Merino sheep flourished in Vermont from 1830 to 1850 where they took many prizes. Jarvis died at the age of 89 having been a political and financial leader in the town of Weathersfield, an influential leader of the Whig party, and nationally known as an advocate for high protective tariffs.

—R.L.

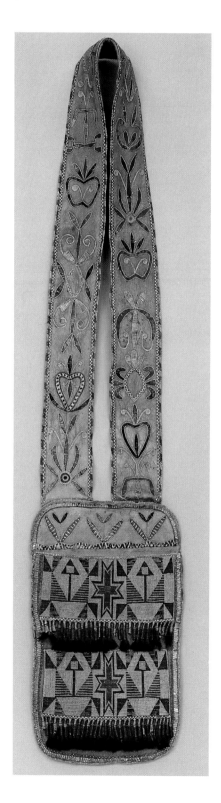

Figure 51.
PA-TUS-SE-NON (SHOT BAG), 1810
Lizette Harmon, Cree Indian, 1790–1862
Porcupine quills, red floss, beads, leather
H: 11 in. W: 7 in.
Gift of Mrs. Nelson Bradley Cramer

Daniel William Harmon was the fourth son of Captain Daniel Harmon and Lucretia Dewey, niece of the Reverend Jedediah Dewey, first minister of the Old First Church in Bennington, and keeper of the Harmon Inn, one of the area's earliest taverns. Harmon was born on February 19, 1798, at the tavern located two miles west of today's Bennington Monument. Travelers to and from Montreal often stopped there. These Canadians may have had a profound influence on the boy who spent, subsequently, most of his life in Canada where, as an authorized agent working for the Northwest Trading Company, he supervised the trading of merchandise.

In 1805, as was customary at the time, Harmon "took a squaw," Elizabeth (Lizette) Laval, daughter of a French Canadian voyageur and a Cree Indian who bore him ten children. When Harmon returned to Vermont, he legitimized their union through marriage, something that was not customary in the backwoods where men could, and did, leave their wives at any time.

This shot bag was made by Lizette for her husband and was decorated with naturally-dyed porcupine quills. Although shot bags do survive, few can be found with leather in such fine condition, with such vibrant colors still evident, or with such strong documentation and history.

—R.L.

Fig. 51

Fig. 52

Figure 52.
SAMPLER, ca. 1798
Betsy Fifield Bean
American, born 1786
Silk on linsey-woolsey
H: 24½ in. W: 17½ in.
Gift of Dr. Donna K. McCurdy

This sampler was worked by Betsy F. Bean, who was born in Salisbury, N.H. on May 21, 1786, and was probably completed when she was 12, the average age for such an accomplishment. While many samplers can be identified with specific regions, schools, or teachers of ornamental needlework, this unique sampler does not closely resemble any known style.

Early Colonial samplers were strongly influenced by European needlework traditions, but by the mid-18th century distinct regional styles had developed in America, primarily in and around urban centers such as Boston, Charlestown, Newport and Philadelphia. After the Revolution, increased prosperity and a growing emphasis on education led to the establishment of many schools and academies throughout the nation. Girls were instructed in a variety of subjects, but usually had to demonstrate proficiency in needlework before their education was considered complete. Working a sampler was both an exercise and a symbol of this achievement which was often framed and proudly hung in the family's home where its skill and artistry could be admired. The sampler also served as a record of stitches, which could be consulted by a girl in her later life when her responsibilities would require her to sew, mend and decorate clothing and household textiles.

Joseph and Elizabeth Fifield Bean, both of Scottish descent, were early settlers of Salisbury, N.H. Active in town government and a very wealthy property-owner, Joseph Bean gave a farm to each of his five children. Although little is known about his daughter's life, records indicate Betsy was the second-born, and married Durrell Elliot from the neighboring town of Boscowen.

While the whimsical and somewhat naive style of Betsy's sampler suggests it was an independent effort, it is probably more likely that she received private instruction at home. The sampler was worked in a variety of stitches with over a dozen different colors of silk thread, many of which could have been purchased locally. The background material is a hand-woven combination of linen and wool threads called linsey-woolsey which was rarely used in samplers, appearing occasionally between 1798–1832 in Philadelphia; Portsmouth and Dover, N.H., and in a scattering of other towns in New England and Canada.

The sampler follows a standard format: rows of alphabets and numerals, a section of pictorial decoration, and a verse. Sampler verses were taken from the Bible, popular hymns, school primers and poetry of the day and most were meditations on love and virtue (especially patience) or reflections on the brevity of life and imminence of death. In this verse, Betsy (or Eliza) sees her own life "speed away" in the looking-glass.

The profusion of decorative motifs shows little kinship to other samplers of this period from New Hampshire. The crowned lions and rows of stylized carnations are part of the English tradition. Some of the borderwork resembles Scotch-Irish weave structures. The hearts, perched birds and baskets of flowers are common to samplers from many regions, but the owls and peacocks are seen less frequently. The most intriguing component of this sampler is the large central design around which a menagerie of animals is arranged. It might represent a female figure with apron, shawl and headpiece, perhaps one of Betsy's female relatives or Betsy herself. As yet, no counterpart to this design is known, and its significance remains a mystery.

—L.J.G.

Figure 53.
WASP TOURING CAR, 1925
The Martin Wasp Corporation
Bennington, Vermont
Gift of Mr. Henry Dodge

Karl Martin realized an ambition of long standing when he produced the first Wasp touring car which was the culmination of a design and engineering experience that began when Martin became a professional designer and builder of automobile coach-work in 1912. Even while serving in the Naval Aviation Department during World War I, Martin pursued automotive design work and after his discharge from the Navy in 1919, he moved to Bennington where he began construction of the first of a group of six cars.

The first Wasp, barely completed in time for National Automobile Week in New York, was exhibited at the Commodore Hotel in January, 1920. It was received by the public with enthusiasm for its startling and unusual design and fine craftsmanship. Douglas Fairbanks Sr., upon seeing the car, bought it on the spot.

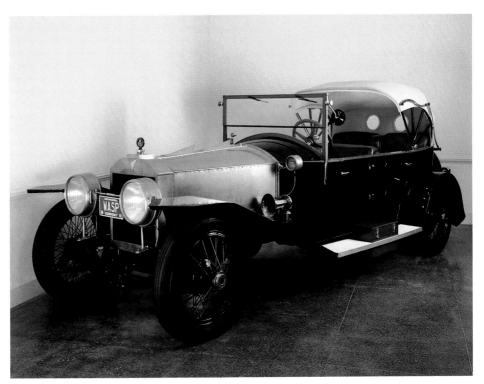

Fig. 53

Spectacular in appearance, the Wasp was constructed of the finest materials and components available. A Wisconsin T head engine, such as powered the Stutz with a Bosch ignition, powered the car. A chrome nickel, heat treated frame on Timkin axles combined with Rudge Whitworth wire wheels gave the car strength, stability and speed. For the 1924 season a Continental six-cylinder engine of greater power was combined with a four speed transmission with overdrive which, on the fourth speed, gave the car quietness and smoothness at even higher speeds. The coachwork was crafted in Bennington under the careful, direct supervision of Karl Martin.

As a result of monetary problems and slow sales due to a post war business slump, the company failed and the last Wasp, now displayed in The Bennington Museum, was produced in 1925. Although the company lingered on, producing custom wood-work and special castings, its doors closed permanently in 1932, a sad end to Vermont's first true automobile manufacturing company, the total production of which was only 16 cars. While only a small number when compared to the giants of the industry, it is quite creditable considering that many companies produced only one or two cars.

—E.K.

Fig. 54

Figure 54.
CARVED EAGLE, early 19th century
American
Gilded pine; reinforced with wrought iron straps
H: 29 in. W: 60 in.
Gift of Hall Park McCullough

Carved gravestones, mastheads, shop-signs and other advertising figures, along with architectural ornamentation, were the earliest forms of sculpture in America. This vigorous and fierce-appearing eagle, symbol of the young American republic, was probably carved in the early 1800s. For many years it has been attributed to Simeon Skillin, Sr. (1716–1778) or one of his sons, the most prominent carvers in Boston in the second half of the 18th century. These craftsmen were of such distinction that they represented the carver's trade in a procession of artisans, tradesmen and manufacturers celebrating George Washington's first visit to Boston as President in November of 1789. Current scholarship suggests, however, that the naturalistic and expressive nature of this carving distinguishes it from the work of the Skillins, who produced more emblematic figures, and that it may be the work instead, of a carver who trained at the Skillin workshop (at least one journeyman who worked for the Skillins in the 1790s left for the West Indies and his work has never been documented), or perhaps studied with William Rush (1756–1833) of Philadelphia. An eagle made by Rush in circa 1810 (now in the collection of the Pennsylvania Academy of the Fine Arts), of similar size, nobility and grandeur, may have been the inspiration for this carving. Although the maker of this eagle is as yet unidentified, its use is clear. It was made to be seen from below, undoubtedly to be hung on a high wall or over the doorway of a public building. According to tradition, this sculpture once graced a structure in Newport, Rhode Island.

—C.Z.

Fig. 55.

Figure 55.
CANNON, 3-Pound, 1776
J & P Verbruggen (1770–1886), Woolwich (now a borough of London), England
Overall L: 41 in.
Gunmetal Bronze
Molded on breech ring: "I & P VERBRUGGEN FECERVUNT. A. 1776."; weight stamped on breech: "I : 3 : 17" ; between trunnions: a broad arrow (noting military ownership)

This gun is one of the four cannons taken on August 16, 1777, by General Stark's troops at The Battle of Bennington. The guns were practically new having been cast the year before by Jan and Pieter Verbruggen at Woolwich (now a borough of London) and were probably used for the rest of the Revolutionary War by American forces. It is known that the cannons were used during the War of 1812 when two of them were captured by the British at the American surrender of Detroit on August 6, 1812, only to be recaptured by the Americans at Fort George on the Niagara River in May of the following year. At the conclusion of the War two of the cannons were placed in an ordinance depot in Washington where they were later declared obsolete. In 1848, Congress ordered them sent to the Watervliet Arsenal near Troy, New York, where they were given new carriages for presentation to the State of Vermont.

That same year Henry B. Stevens, antiquarian, historian and founder of the Vermont Historical Society, received the two cannon for Vermont from the United States Government. They were briefly exhibited in Bennington on August 16, 1848, in celebration of the 71st anniversary of the Battle of Bennington after which they were returned to Montpelier. One cannon was placed at the State House there and the second, this one, in The Bennington Museum for the Museum's opening in 1928.

Fig. 56

The Museum's cannon, specially engraved for its return to Vermont "TAKEN/ FROM THE/GERMANS/AT BENNINGTON/AUG. 16, 1777.," is a well preserved example of 18th century cannon founders' art. The carriage mount reflects the state of the art in 1848, and is essentially the same design which was used throughout the Civil War by both the North and the South.

—E.K.

Figure 56.
TOYS AND DOLLS, 19th Century
Various manufacturers
Bennington, North Bennington, Springfield, Vermont; Pennsylvania; New York; France
Iron, tin, wood, paper, bisque, leather, wool, cotton
Museum collection, Gift of Mrs. Joseph Wilson, Sr., Mr. and Mrs. Harry Breese, Miss Lois Higbie, Mrs. Philip E. Adams, Mrs. Sarita Weeks, Miss Fanny and Miss Ruth Carrier, Mrs. Margery Ludlow

During the 19th century the toy industry in America saw rapid development. As a result of mass production and new materials adapted to toymaking, a remarkable diversity of playthings were manufactured in great numbers and at affordable prices. The country's general prosperity gave people the means to purchase objects solely for entertainment, and attitudes towards children changed. The view of children as miniature adults was replaced by the concept of childhood, seen as an idyllic period before adulthood to be filled with imaginative play, and carefully tempered with games intended to educate and edify.

One of the first materials used for mass-produced toys in the 1840s was tin, a lightweight, inexpensive and malleable metal. A countless variety of toys, such as the mechanical frog shown here, were stamped out of tin sheets, shaped and decorated.

However, beginning in the 1870s cast iron was used extensively to make more durable toys from reusable molds. Cast-iron mechanical banks, miniature stoves, kitchenware and toy vehicles of all kinds were popular for many years. By the 1880s, toy manufacturers used lithography to transfer elaborate, multi-colored designs to paper, which was then glued to wooden forms to create doll houses, game boards, puzzles, blocks, and toy trains and boats.

A profusion of educational games appeared during the 19th century in response to the emphasis on the nurturing atmosphere of the home and the importance of learning. "Grandma's Game of Useful Knowledge" tested older children's grasp of academic and moral teaching by posing such questions as "What is flax?" and "When was the world created?" Alphabet blocks allowed younger children to have fun while using their reading skills, and card games taught both children and adults about literature, geography and history.

Dolls were fashioned from a great variety of materials such as corn husks, rubber, papier-mache, wool, from scraps of fabric and printed cloth patterns, and from wood. One of the very first mass-produced dolls in America was a jointed wooden doll, as seen here, patented in 1873 by Joel Ellis of Springfield, Vt. Despite the increase in the number of American-made dolls, imported bisque and china dolls from Germany and France continued to be popular, such as the delicately featured Jumeau Bebe doll shown in the illustration.

While toys have always been a part of children's lives, it was not until the 19th century that such an abundance and variety of objects were designed specifically to create and fill a child's world.

—L.J.G.

Figure 57.
TERRESTRIAL GLOBE, 1810
James Wilson
American, 1763–1855
Hand-colored engraving on paper on wood and plaster form
Mahogany stand with four turned legs
C: 41½ in.
Gift of Hall Park McCullough Fund

James Wilson of Bradford, Vt., a successful farmer and blacksmith, but a man of little formal education, became fascinated by geography and exploration. At 37 years of age, with a farm to run and children to support, he set forth to make globes as fine as those imported from England, and at a price village schools could afford. Wilson knew nothing of geography and cartography, or of astronomy and mathematics, but was determined to learn. In order to acquire the knowledge necessary to produce an accurate globe, Wilson purchased the 1797 eighteen-volume set of Encyclopaedia Britannica for the sum of $130, and also tried his hand at the difficult art of engraving. Unable to master this technique, Wilson traveled 250 miles on foot to New Haven, Ct., where he studied with the well-known engraver/cartographer, Amos Doolittle, engraver of the first maps to be published in the earliest known geography book in America.

By January of 1810, Wilson had sold "A New Terrestrial Globe, on Which the Facts & New Discoveries Are Laid Down from the Accurate Observations Made by Capts. Cook, Furneux, Phipps, etc." Wilson made globes for more than 50 years and experimented with many different models of the sun and earth and, in this sense, took part in the great explorations of the time. Although Wilson was married three times,

Fig. 57

fathered ten children, and worked the family farm, he was also self-educated. Today Wilson is renowned not only for making the first globe in the United States but also, with the help of his sons, for producing globes which changed the way Americans and others viewed the world.

—R.L.

Figure 58.
DALMATIAN DOG, one of a pair
Mid to Late 19th century
Possibly Gray Foundry, Poultney, Vermont
Cast Iron
H: 2½ ft. L: 4 ft.
Gift of Robert J. M. Matteson in Memory of Peleg and Mollie Matteson

Two life-size, cast-iron Dalmatian dogs stood for 50 years on the lawn at 318 South Street in Bennington, Vt., the home of Dr. and Mrs. Peleg Matteson, parents of the donor. According to family tradition, the dogs were cast at a foundry built in 1828 in Poultney, Vt. on an industrial site which had been established in 1811. In 1829, fire

Fig. 58

destroyed all but the foundry which went on to become well-known for the production of fine patented, cast-iron stoves. In 1844, the foundry was purchased by Henry J. Ruggles whose family operated it until 1900 after which it was known as the Gray Iron Works, recognized for the production of slate sawing and planing machines. In the early 1960s the Foundry closed its doors due to foreign competition and environmental controls, and today the buildings no longer exist.

Dogs such as these Dalmatians became popular in the mid-19th century when the use of stags, floral forms, dogs and other animals were widely used as decorative forms in response to America's desire to emulate British taste. Foundries in Europe as well as in America responded to this increased demand and decorative pieces were produced in great variety and number to adorn formal gardens and lawns. Dalmatians, long known as "Coach dogs" were adopted by American firemen as their mascot explaining why they are known today as Firehouse Dogs.

Despite family tradition, current scholarship suggests these dogs date more accurately from the end of the 19th century and, at present, there is no way of determining where the dogs were cast.

—R.L.

Fig. 59

Figure 59.
VERMONT HAND TOOLS, 19th c.
Hawes patent square, 1823, price $5.00 Shaftsbury
Breast drill, ca. 1860 A.W. Whitney, Woodstock
Plow plane, 1844, E. Dutcher, Pownal
Toy square, ca. 1850, B. Harmon, North Bennington
Drawshave, ca. 1860 L.F. Bailey, South Ryegate
Tongue plane, ca. 1862, E.S. Pierce, Jr., Jamaica
Gift of Paul Kebabian

Early American tools made in Vermont are of special interest because the firms that made them were, with a few exceptions, quite small and the number of tools made was also relatively small. This limited production, coupled with normal wear and loss over a century or more of use, explains the scarcity of Vermont tools.

The metallic plow plane patented and made by Shaftsbury-born Elihu Dutcher in 1844, while a much more durable tool than, for instance, a wooden rule, was made in such limited quantities that it is very rare today. Serving as a Baptist minister in Pownal, Vt., Dutcher supplemented his income by building carriages and wagons for which he used the plow plane to fit the door and side panels. As such, the plane was readily adopted by carpenters and cabinetmakers and soon became copied by others making it unlikely that Dutcher made much money on his invention.

Carpenters' framing squares have been an important regional product, having been made in Bennington and Shaftsbury since Silas Hawes of Shaftsbury received his patent in 1819. At least 15 individual firms have made squares in these towns since that time. The merger of four of the larger firms in 1858 formed the Eagle Square Company in Shaftsbury and effectively ended the era of the small individual makers. Forged of iron and steel, many squares survive today but those by earlier makers are increasingly rare. Considering local square production from 1800 to the present, Bennington and Shaftsbury have long been the world center of the square-making industry producing a tool used in constructing most of the buildings in North

America. In 1916, the Eagle Square Company was purchased by the Stanley Rule and Level Company and it is still in operation today.

The breast drill made in about 1860 by A. W. Whitney of Woodstock, Vt. is made of cast-iron, the spindle made of steel with a tapered bore to hold tapered shank bits. Whitney, in business from 1852 to 1870, also patented and made a line of tinsmiths' tools.

The tongue plane made by E. S. Pierce Jr. of Jamaica, Vt. between 1861 and 1864 is similar to those made by other Vermont planemakers as well as by planemakers throughout the entire northeast. Relatively few planes bearing the mark of a Vermont maker exist today.

L. F. Bailey of South Ryegate made this tool handle drawshave in about 1860. Sharpened only on the curve and the straight right hand edge, it is a special tool to facilitate the production of a variety of round or oval tool handles made of wood.

In the last half of the 19th century, the Douglass Manufacturing Company and the Arlington Edge Tool Company made thousands of chisels in the eastern part of Arlington, Vt. an area still called Chiselville. Perhaps more chisels are ruined by abuse, accident and neglect than are worn out by use and sharpening. As a consequence few of the Arlington-made chisels survive to this day. The Vermont tools which have been identified are important links between the craftsmen and the homes, barns and furniture they produced, and are highly valued today.

—E.K.

Figure 60.
TANKARD, ca. 1690–1700
Jacobus van der Spiegel, 1668–1708
New York
Silver H: 5¾ in.
Gift of Grace Seymour Roberts Reynolds

LADLE, ca. 1820
Unknown maker
Eastern New York State
Silver L: 14 in.
Gift of Laura Van der Spiegel Merrill Penniman

This tankard is the oldest piece of silver in the Museum collection and bears strong Dutch characteristics since its maker, Jacobus van der Spiegel, born in New York, was of Dutch descent. The ladle which was made from the metal of the tankard's cover 125 years later, and not marked, is by an unknown silversmith.

While still a young man, van der Spiegel saw militia service on the Albany frontier, and in 1692 married Anna Sanders in the Albany Dutch Church. Well regarded in New York, he served from 1694 to 1695 as an assessor and in 1698, as a constable. However, when van der Spiegel was made a freeman in February, 1701, he was listed as a silversmith and, unfortunately, died at the comparatively young age of 40 in 1708. His work today is very scarce in view of his short working life and, over the years, much has doubtless been lost or melted down to make new objects.

Tankards made in New York, originally a Dutch settlement, were strongly influenced by Dutch silversmithing traditions and often were elaborately engraved, with applied cast decoration and elaborate base bands, and a rather low profile. These characteristics set New York silver apart from the silver of other American cities. This tankard, formerly owned by Jacobus van der Spiegel's brother, Hendrick, bears a skillfully engraved decorative crest or coat of arms of the van der Spiegel family. A cast

Fig. 60

relief ornament, a "lion couchant," is placed on the handle just below the hinge, and the lower end of the handle bears a disc on which is placed a cast cherub's head. The base band of repeated stamped or rolled designs is indicative of New York silver of the period, below which is a line of applied meander wire, the details of which are almost lost due to repeated polishing.

One can only surmise what the design of the cover was when it was removed in about 1820 to be converted into the ladle shown with the tankard. A script cypher LVDS for Laura van der Spiegel, its owner, appears on the handle and the tankard bears the letters HVPS, for Hendrick van der Spiegel, on the handle below the lion. The tankard descended through the van der Spiegel family to a branch in Bennington and was presented to the Museum by a great-great-great granddaughter in 1951. The ladle was given to the Museum in 1966 by a direct descendant of the family.

—E.K.

Figure 61.
TILT-TOP TABLE, 1762
Paintings, ca. 1920
Anna Mary Robertson Moses (Grandma Moses)
American, 1860–1961
Pine planks, painted with oils
H: 27½ in. W: 45 in. D: 31½ in.
Painted on the base of table: THE OLD MCMURRY/DINING TABLE/MADE FOR THE/OLD LOG HOUSE/1762
Museum Purchase

Anna Mary Robertson was born in Easton, N.Y., near Greenwich on September 7,

Fig. 61

1860, and spent her early life as a hired girl before her marriage in 1887 to Thomas Salmon Moses. Known as "Grandma Moses" she began to paint seriously in 1930 at the age of 70, after the death of her husband, and soon was exhibiting her work at the local drugstore, and selling paintings at county fairs where she priced them according to their size.

Although far from being topographically correct, Grandma Moses' paintings recall her childhood and the many routines and activities of farm life as well as such traditional events as sugaring off, or maple sugaring. Her paintings, filled with people, houses, barns, farm animals and household pets were a celebration of life as she saw it, a life that for Grandma Moses was to last 101 years.

Today she is not only a well-known and much revered artist but an American folk hero whose work represents an earlier time and a simpler way of life. Grandma Moses wrote "I looked back on my life like a good day's work. It was done and I feel satisfied with it. I was happy and contented. I knew nothing better and made the best out of what life offered. Life is what we make it, always has been, always will be."

This 18th century wooden table, called by Grandma Moses a "tip-up" table, was given to her by an aunt. She used it as an easel and decorated each side with one of her own paintings. The six landscapes on this table emphasize Grandma Moses' strong attachment to the countryside in her life and work.

—R.L.

Fig. 62

Figure 62.
FLATWARE, 1840–1865
Roswell H. Bailey (1804–1886)
Woodstock, Vermont
Silver
All marked: R.H. BAILEY, and some additionally: WOODSTOCK
Gift of Lilian Baker Carlisle

During Vermont's early years, few of the territory's inhabitants could afford the luxury of owning silver. These first settlers focused their attention on more practical concerns such as clearing land for farming and defending their property. It was not until the early 19th century that numbers of craftsmen from Massachusetts, Connecticut and New York, moved to Vermont to establish shops where they regularly made and repaired watches, clocks and jewelry as well as silver teaspoons and tablespoons. On the frontier, one had to be versatile to earn a living; and in addition to silversmithing, it was not uncommon for craftsmen to work as innkeepers, postmasters, town clerks, dentists, druggists or photographers to support their families.

By the mid-19th century, the population of Vermont had increased dramatically and many were prospering. Not surprisingly, all but the smallest settlements in Vermont had a resident silversmith, clock and watch repairer and/or jeweler by this time. However, the mainstay of the local silversmith's production was not showy hollowware, but simple flatware which was in greater demand.

Two of the most prolific silversmiths in Vermont were Roswell J. Bailey (1804–1886) of Woodstock, Vermont, the maker of the flatware shown here, and his distant cousin Bradbury M. Bailey (1824–1913). Roswell Bailey advertised the sale of tea, table, dessert, salt and mustard spoons, cream ladles, sugar tongs and butter knives, and the repair of spoons and spectacles. The objects shown here, are from left to right: a teaspoon with swaged handle; fiddle handle teaspoon; tip'd handle teaspoon; sugar shell; tablespoon; dessert spoon; cream or gravy ladle; (and below) a

Fig. 63

sugar shovel, salt spoon and tea knife with pearl handle. These objects constitute a
small but significant part of the Museum's collection of Vermont silver which includes
the work of almost sixty makers, among them: Abram, Edgar and William Brinsmaid
of Burlington, Levi Pitkin and Ira S. Town of Montpelier, and William Johonnot of
Windsor. As such, it is the largest public collection in the state.

—C.Z.

Figure 63.
VERMONT PAPER AND COPPER CURRENCY, 1781, and 1785 to 1788
Spooner & Green, printers
Reuben Harmon, minter
Westminster and Rupert, Vermont
Paper, copper
Anonymous Gift and McCullough-Vlack coin collection

To meet the costs generated by the Revolutionary War, the original 13 states were
forced to issue paper currency. As a result, in 1781, Vermont joined the states in
producing a comparatively small issue of paper currency, consisting of only 25,155
pounds value in legal tender Bills of Credit. The bills, in eight different denominations, were redeemable for silver at six shillings, eight pence per ounce until 1782 after
which they were receivable for taxes. The nearly complete redemption of the notes
and the fact that they were printed on thin, weak paper accounts for their great rarity
today. Few survive in good condition and most have been repaired, including bills
which were actually sewn together with needle and thread. All of the notes required
the signature of two of the four signers appointed by the legislature, one of whom was
Ebenezer Walbridge of Bennington. His desk, now in the Museum collection, may
have been the one on which he signed the notes.

Shortly after the paper currency was issued, counterfeits began to appear despite the stern warning, "Death To Counterfeit," printed on the back of all notes. Accusations were lodged against the printers, Spooner & Green, until one of the employees of the shop was found to be guilty of the crime.

Because the National Government had not yet begun to strike coins, there was a shortage of metallic currency necessary to conduct everyday business in America. In an effort to alleviate this shortage several of the states in the Northeast authorized the striking of coins and, although not yet officially a state, Vermont was the earliest to do so. In June, 1785, the Vermont legislature authorized Reuben Harmon of Rupert, Vt. to make copper coins for a period of two years. In October, 1786, a second legislature extended the authorization for an additional eight years, and also stipulated a change in design. The coins of Vermont are, as a result, of two quite different and distinct designs.

The first design, on the obverse, shows the sun rising over a distant tree-covered mountain with the plow as a symbol of husbandry and peace in the foreground, and the entire coin surrounded by the Latin words Vermontensum Res. Publica (The Republic of Vermont). There are a total of three variations in the Latin spelling of Vermont on the first coins that were struck. The reverse of these coins bears an eye within a small circle surrounded by 26 alternating long and short rays encircled by 13 stars and the legend "Stella Quarta Decima" (The Fourteenth Star), signifying Vermont's aspiration to become the fourteenth state. During 1786 the design required by the State Legislature appeared which was similar to the design used on English pennies in common circulation at the time. This second design featured an artist's rendition of a portrait bust symbolizing authority with the words "Vermon Auctori" (By Authority of Vermont) and on the reverse side a seated female figure holding an olive branch in her right hand, a staff in her left hand, and a shield on the ground. Around the edge of the coin are the words "Inde et Lib" (Independence and Liberty) with the date under the shield. The last Vermont coins were struck in 1788 as a result of a decrease in the value of copper and rising costs of production although they remained in circulation for many years.

All eight denominations of Vermont paper currency are extremely rare today. Vermont coins, although less perishable, are still not common but exist in greater numbers. Both currencies are highly-prized numismatic examples of Vermont's turbulent struggle as an independent republic aspiring to statehood.

—E.K.

Figure 64.
BENNINGTON BATTLE FLAG, 1776
Sewn by the women of Bennington, Vermont
Cotton
5½ ft. × 10 ft.
Gift of Maude Fillmore Wilson

Acknowledged as the oldest known Stars and Stripes, this unusually large flag is thought to have flown over General Stark's encampment during the Battle of Bennington. A unique interpretation of the Stars and Stripes, the flag is related in concept and design to other historical regimental flags where emphasis was placed on the field and arrangement of the stars. The striking "arch" form as well as the unique seven pointed stars may have Masonic significance. The stripes follow the heraldic order

Fig. 64

frequently used during the Revolutionary period, alternating white and red, instead of
the red and white of more recent American flags.

According to tradition, the flag was woven in the village of Old Bennington with
linen flax from the area. However, more recent study of the fibers establishes that the
fabric is in fact cotton. It is clear that the women who made it took pride in their work;
among them was the grandmother of future United States president Millard Fillmore,
Hepzebah, wife of Lieutenant Nathaniel Fillmore, one of the heroes of the Battle of
Bennington and the man who saved the flag. It was in the possession of Lt. Fillmore
until 1812 when he gave it to his nephew Septa Fillmore, who passed the flag on to the
son of the famous architect, Lavius Fillmore. It remained in the Fillmore family until
1926 when the flag was given to the Bennington Battle Monument and Historical
Association (now The Bennington Museum), by Maude Fillmore Wilson.

—R.L.

INDEX